eureka!

This book is dedicated to Gary Thomas and Tim Shore, with thanks for their support and good humour. Cofiwch.

Special thanks to Stephan Stockton, my collaborator on the eureka workshops, and to all you adventurous people who came on the first workshops in Cardiff. A big thankyou, too, to Sam and Andy Johnson for the illustrations.

I would like to thank editors Emma Heyworth-Dunn and Jacqui Lewis for all the thoroughness and commitment they have brought to working on this book. Thanks too, to Rowena Webb and Hodder Mobius, and my agent Vicki McIvor.

Philippa Davies can be reached at
www.philippadavies.co.uk

Contents

Introduction

Do you recall the story of King Hiero and Archimedes? King Hiero had a crown and he wanted to know what it was made of – whether it was made of gold or silver alloy. So he asked Archimedes, who was known to be sharp, to figure out a way of working out this problem. Archimedes had been musing over this question for a while and, one evening (he had just submerged himself into a deep bath of water), inspiration struck. He realized that the volume of water, which had splashed over the top of his bath, was equal to his size. So if he plunged first the crown, followed by a gold ingot of the same weight, into the bath, and they both displaced the same volume of water, then the crown was pure gold. According to legend, so excited was Archimedes with his idea, that he rushed stark naked out into the street, shouting 'eureka!' – which is Greek for 'I've got it!'

Now, much as I love the idea of hordes of you readers rushing out into the street, stark naked, and shouting 'By Jove, I've got it!', that's not exactly what's on offer here. This book is about how you generate brilliant ideas and make them happen. It's about projects you want to effect: in business – your own or other people's; in improving public sector organizations; or as part of your dream of your ideal life – like writing a novel or setting up a charity. We all know people who have great ideas, and talk about them, but never seem to bring them to fruition. This book tackles the barriers that prevent these ideas from happening, like low confidence, lack of inspiration, sensitivity to criticism and poor selling skills. It describes a totally new way of looking at these issues, based on really up-to-date knowledge about how our minds work. But it is also very, very practical. The eureka programme describes, phase by phase, how you can make your brilliant ideas happen, wherever your aspirations lie.

Writing this book has been very exciting, thanks to new insights from neuroscience and psychology. For a long time, I have been fascinated by the way people get ideas and use their imaginations. These are the sources of most human achievement, yet relatively little interesting investigation has been done into them. But these new insights have shed light on how the unconscious mind works, in a way that is rather different from the one Freud described. How your unconscious and conscious minds communicate is a vital part of generating ideas, and one that we investigate thoroughly in *eureka*.

I realized too, through research into exceptionally creative people, that these people were using their minds in very specific ways – ways that were not covered by definitions of traditional intelligence, or even emotional or spiritual intelligence. People like Madonna, James Dyson, Anita Roddick and Walt Disney had distinctive approaches and attitudes to life. They were using their minds and whole beings differently – in such a distinctive manner that it deserved to be described as its own intelligence: creative intelligence. I put these findings into practice on pilot eureka workshops, with people from all walks of life – managers, entrepreneurs, scientists, artists, writers, educators and various professionals – and this book is the result of this research and these experiments. It tells their story. What I discovered through these workshops was that the skills of creative intelligence could be applied to any context: business, administration, art or science.

Eureka answers the question: why do some people make

their ideas happen, while others just dream? It takes you on a journey, which starts with examining your potential to make ideas happen; moves on to how you can build creative intelligence through tuning into your unconscious, using a specific creative process, and 'soft' thinking skills; and concludes with how best to involve others in making brilliant ideas happen – through selling your ideas effectively, creative teamwork and understanding the influences that create epidemic popularity.

On offer, here, are two approaches. The first concerns itself with the mindset of creative intelligence and answers the question: how do you change your orientation so that you become more creative – permanently? This approach changes the way people see the world, through shifting perception and habits. I am interested in applied psychology: how theory creates practice, and so the framework of eureka is about what you can *do* to make your brilliant ideas happen. All the chapters of this book relate to a specific process of building creative intelligence, described in detail in Chapter One. This involves the actions of believing, immersing, idea-generating, creating a vision, reality-checking, piloting and realising. As you shall see, this process is a circular, cyclical one, rather than one that can neatly be described in a straight line, stage-by-stage. I've indicated, at the start of each chapter, where it takes us in this process.

You could be reading this book because you want to create or invent something yourself, start a competitive business, write a screenplay, build an innovative team, solve public sector problems or help others develop their creativity. You could be reading it just because such subjects interest you, or because they ran out of the latest Patricia Cornwell at the airport. Either way, the eureka programme sections that run through this book will help you put the many ideas here into practice.

The Bit About Me

While creativity involves convention-breaking, there is only so far you can go. Those of you who love self-development books will know it is standard procedure for the author to convey some of their own story in them, so here goes:

A few years ago, a client asked me to design a course for people who felt they were at a crossroads in their lives. I thought I'd get people to draw themselves in a picture of their lives, rather than talk about themselves – not a particularly original or new approach in my sort of work. I was amazed at the results. With a bit of encouragement, my workshop participants drew really evocative and full pictures of what was happening in their lives. For the self-effacing, especially, it seemed much easier to describe their situations with a picture. They spoke paragraphs about themselves as they described what the pictures meant – in marked contrast with the terse one-line introductions most of them had made at the beginning of the day. The pictures seemed to bring out conflicts and concerns from people, many of which were unconscious, like those done by the woman who drew herself as a tiny figure surrounded by family members and work colleagues who were on a massive scale . . .

Around the same time, I was hired by British Airways to help with a big redundancy programme they were running. Understandably, attendees at those workshops were often quite traumatized about being made redundant. My task was to prepare them to talk about themselves confidently at job interviews. I hit upon the idea of teaching them about story structure and how to tell effective stories, and then to use these guidelines for talking about their lives. The effect was dramatic: the anxious, the tongue-tied and the angry suddenly found a means of selling themselves at interviews.

Participants told me they loved these workshops, finding

them immensely helpful, and it sparked my interest in creativity. I held both arts and science degrees and was always interested in the overlap between the two. I set myself to designing courses that used arty movie-acting techniques known as 'the Method', which were combined with scientific approaches to peak performance from sports psychology. I started to find lots of parallels between artistic and scientific approaches to human behaviour. My enthusiasm for my business was infectious, and when we started to get clients like Prime Ministers, cabinet ministers and blue chip CEOs, we could offer them scientific technical approaches, or much more creative 'interpretative' ones. In order to learn to perform well in front of audiences or on television, they could choose to learn how to change their voices or body language on a technical level, or to method act like Al Pacino.

When I started academic research for a PhD in creativity, I just knew I had to write this book. I wanted to develop the ideas of creative intelligence so that one day it would feature on every school curriculum in the land. I wanted to bring the techniques and research to you, the general public.

And For You

Eureka will take you on a journey from generating the first sparks of ideas, to realising them practically, then on to selling them to others, ending with suggestions for taking your ideas to a larger market. We will start by looking at your area of interest and how wholehearted you are about this area – wholeheartedness being very necessary if you are to make ideas happen. We will examine the considerable power of your unconscious mind, and look at ways of practically accessing this, in the light of new research. In the chapters on creating a vision and critical demons, we will consider the tricky business of balancing a vision with the need to keep in frequent contact with reality. Timing will be of the essence here. Many a visionary has never reached their vision of Planet Blue Sky because someone interfered on the way . . . We will look at how ingrained patterns of thinking and feeling can stop us from having ideas, and investigate ways of retraining our minds and spirits to be more creative.

Then we will investigate psychological idea-throttlers. Our own gremlins can be destructive self-criticism, fear of failure and lack of self-belief. We may also have to deal with individuals who see it as their life mission to pour scorn and discouragement on other people's ideas. We look at tactics for overcoming and silencing negativity – our own and other people's. One of the key factors in people who are successful creatively is the extent to which they engage with the opinions of others and how they use criticism and feedback. For many of us, understandably, these are very sensitive subjects. So in this book, I describe ways you can learn to, love criticism, use it successfully . . . and even become addicted to it. This will not turn you into a masochist, I promise.

While you are reading this book, you will find many myths about creativity and ideas debunked. In groups, for instance, brainstorming rarely works very effectively; it favours only people who are comfortable engaging their mouths at very short notice, sometimes with their brains trailing behind. We will look into the influences that help and hinder groups and teams to create, and investigate how unconscious responses to each other can mar group effectiveness.

And last, but very much not least, we look at how to sell ideas, because, in today's world, however brilliant your idea and what you make with it, if it ain't sold well, it ain't gonna happen. So we end with ideas to make you into a salesperson, even if in your wildest dreams you have never ever seen yourself as such. We will look at how you can communicate and sell yourself so that all interactions, both conscious and unconscious, between yourself and others, assists your aims. We will investigate also, why some ideas become wildly popular, and others don't. And finally, we will look at how we could develop creative potential in the future – in business, government and the public sector, and in how we raise children.

I know this book will give you eureka moments. Just to remind you, the thrill of one of these was so great for Archimedes, that he jumped out of his bath, totally and utterly forgetful of his dangly bits. My hope is that this book will do something similar for you.

1

A Sleeping Giant

This chapter is about believing.

'Imagination is more important than knowledge.' – Einstein

Vicky wants to change her life. She has a good job, which she feels she performs effectively, but something is missing, though she doesn't know what. She has always dreamt of running her own business. Vicky has a holiday scheduled and decides that, rather than escape somewhere scenic, she will stay at home, to try and discover what she might do. She has a hunch that the answer to her dilemma lies in her own mind and in her immediate locality. During her two-week holiday, she potters around locally, chatting to people and thinking about where she lives. She realizes that, to buy top-quality food, or dine out on a decent café lunch, everyone has to jump into their cars. Six months later, around the corner from where she lives, her café-delicatessen 'Vicky's Victuals' opens.

David is applying for his first job, after five years at university. His Master's degree has set him up to specialize in Human Resources and Personnel. He has two job offers: one from a large financial company, and the other from a smaller advertising agency.

The agency enjoys a growing reputation for its 'leading edge' approach and this inspires David. The company has just three layers of employees: account teams, directors and CEO (Chief Executive Officer). On his first day on the job, David is surprised to be told by the CEO that the main purpose of his new role is to work out the answer to the questions: 'How can I make myself redundant in this role, so that my responsibilities go elsewhere? and What else would I like to do in the agency?' On the second day, he is even more surprised to be told by Sally, his director, that his task for the day is to contact all the account clients in order to personally introduce himself to them. Day three finds him going into a state of shock when Sally suggests that, during the weekly communal lunch, he introduce himself to the rest of the company.

'What shall I say?' he gasps.

'Oh I don't know,' says Sally, 'just make it up.'

At the school parents evening, Anna's mum is talking to her teacher. Anna is eight, a very lively child, who constantly makes things at home. As her mother introduces herself, the teacher frowns slightly. 'Yes, Anna's a bright little girl, with plenty to say for herself, as I'm sure you know. I'd just like to get her to stop asking so many questions, especially about *why* we are doing maths, or *why* we need to study comprehension. I mean, there *is* the school curriculum to get through, you know.'

What Vicky and Anna are using, and David is being asked to use, is creativity. They are researching, problem-finding, questioning, following hunches, synthesising and designing. Vicky is identifying a gap in the market and putting this together with her own needs, Anna is being endlessly curious and David is being asked to invent, imagine and 'make things up'. You can probably think of many instances where you have done, or been asked to do, something similar. Whenever you need to be resourceful in life, and to get ideas, you will use your creativity, even though you may not call it that. Instead you may call it 'flying by the seat of your pants'.

Every time you have an idea, make unusual connections, come up with an innovative solution to a problem or act with passion and commitment to inspire and motivate others, you are using your creativity. When you open your mouth to speak – unless you are parroting learnt script – you are being creative. You may not be aware of it, but you will use creativity in designing your home, dreaming up an experimental supper, inventing games with children or just coming up with something interesting to do over a wet weekend. Sometimes it gets called flair, inspiration or resourcefulness. It is linked inextricably to what motivates you and how you learn, and, if you are lucky, you will be called upon to use it a lot at work. Creativity is what keeps organizations and business growing, and gives them a competitive edge. It is our ideas that make things tick.

Genius Potential

All of us are creative and capable of producing great ideas, though we may not believe it to be the case. This chapter covers your beliefs about creativity, and those of other people. During the writing of this book, attendees at workshops would occasionally ask me whether I was writing about any particular subject. When I replied 'creativity,' I usually got the response 'oh dear, I'm not at all creative'. Yet, when I asked the person whether they had any passions or strong interests in life, and what was it about these interests that turned them on, they would talk with inspiration about their love of Thai cooking, football coaching, home design or doing hardcore DIY. They would talk about making or improving something, in a way that clearly gave them great satisfaction.

The urge to create is at the core of what makes us human and it is one of the big distinguishing differences that makes us members of the dominant species on this planet. Creativity occurs in both arts and science, although you probably find more self-consciousness about 'being creative' in the arts. We love to make things and to exchange what we have made with other people for different things – in other words, to trade. And we have been creating things for about 50,000 years. Richard Klein, an anthropologist, identified the foxp2 gene, which mutated around that time, prior to which our development was crude and Stone Age. With the genetic magic of creativity, though, we started to develop language and to produce art and jewellery, the artefacts of style and culture.

Since then, the list of what we have produced is mind-boggling. There's the wheel, electricity, the steam engine, penicillin and the discovery of DNA, to name but a few, plus the Beatles, black holes and Harry Potter, to mention three more. The history of human progress is the history of our brilliant ideas. And these ideas need not be confined to the tangible. The systems that organize us, like democracy and capitalism, evolved out of our ability to create. So, next time your partner moans about the length of time you take to get ready to go out, remind them that this aesthetic sensibility is down to your foxp2 gene – and certainly nothing to do with vanity . . .

Why is it, then, if we all have this creative potential, that so many of us do not realize it? Why aren't we all going about getting brilliant ideas and making them happen? Creativity is often imbued with a sort of mystique, and researchers have puzzled endlessly over what makes creative geniuses different from the rest of us. The truth is that, for the most part, geniuses are just like you and me. As Steven Pinker, the evolutionary psychologist, comments: 'the genius creates good ideas because we all create good ideas.' Genes will play an influence, certainly, but the human brain also demonstrates something that neuroscientists called 'plasticity', which means: the brain changes during learning. When we learn something new, our brains create new neural pathways amongst the hundred billion neurons inside each of our heads.

Michael J.A. Howe, in his book *Genius Explained*, compares genetic advantage with a country that has discovered a mineral, like coal. How it mines and exploits that coal will be critical. When we learn effectively, we mine our genetic inheritance to its fullest potential. The truth is, creative geniuses like Einstein, Darwin, Marie Curie, the Beatles and Bill Gates work longer and harder than the rest of us, and they learn better. They have gigantic amounts of curiosity and commitment. But it's not entirely down to them, of course. Good luck, combined with good judgement, put them in the right place at the right time.

Geniuses have brilliant ideas because they have *more* ideas – and that includes duff ones, too. Many creativity researchers have concluded that it takes about ten years of mastery in a field for exceptional creativity to occur. Even Mozart – who produced thrilling compositions early in his life – was hot-housed by his father from the age of three. He started to produce great work when he was twelve. Much of the time, people get brilliant ideas by sticking at it. They conduct lots of experiments: some of which succeed rather better than others. We often think of geniuses as being relentlessly good at things, but the fact that they fail, too, should be inspiring. We can think: 'if they can do it, so can I'.

Even though the last decade saw great progress in brain research, the subject is still in its infancy. A huge amount still exists to be learned about how the brain works. Very recently, scientists have discovered that eureka moments generate much activity in a part of the brain called the anterior superior gynus, in the right temporal lobe. Freud thought that creativity was a way of dealing with nasty urges like sex and aggression, which we subliminate in our unconscious. He viewed the unconscious as a type of container that repressed these undesirable qualities. According to Adam Philips, Freud's most recent editor, while Freud deserves to be viewed as a great literary figure, we have moved on from some of his ideas. And one of these ideas we have moved on from is his definition of the unconscious.

Traditional Intelligence

Very recent research from the USA says that, yes, the unconscious is mightily powerful; but, rather than being like a container, it acts like a scanner, helping us survive in highly complex and stimulating environments. As a scanner, it helps us see, interpret and survive in the world, without our being aware of it. The unconscious takes in information that feeds our creativity. Whether you've experienced eureka moments or sustained creative periods, you will know that unexpected leaps of connection seem to occur between your unconscious and your conscious mind. Alexander McCall-Smith is a professor of medical law who also writes the bestselling Precious Ramotswe books about a female private detective in Botswana. His stories are currently being made into a film and television series. Quoted in *The Sunday Times*, he explains the 4,000 words he writes every day thus: 'I sit down and there is some inner voice that takes over. I don't have to think about it. It's an odd thing to explain. It is an access to something that is going on in the unconscious.'

You may know too, that if you try very hard and consciously to 'be creative' and come up with good ideas, nothing happens. Your conscious effort can have a stultifying effect, in fact. So creativity involves a very important relationship between our unconscious and conscious levels of thinking, one we will investigate further in Chapter Three.

a sleeping giant

I mentioned earlier that geniuses spend exceptional time and commitment on their chosen area of interest, and many of us may not have had the opportunity or idea of doing this. But we may also be victims of one of the most common, and strangest notions about how our minds work: that they are independent thinking machines separate from our feelings and imaginations. But you will know from experience that your thoughts, feelings and imaginings interact. How much easier is it to study, for instance, when you feel confident and are able to imagine your post-exam euphoria? To what extent are you able to concentrate fully on your work when a close relative is undergoing a serious operation? And this odd notion that thinking exists in some sort of vacuum has meant that a specific type of intelligence has been valued above all others. This type of intelligence involves, above all else, analysis.

Intelligence is most often defined as a form of pattern-detecting, which helps us survive in different environments, and to set goals for ourselves. The traditional definition of intelligence involves analysis through splitting things into their component parts. It is a purely conscious activity. Mechanistic problems like a car engine not working are often easily solved by the informed, which they do by using their IQ (intelligence quotient) – as it is traditionally known. You just take the bits apart, examine each one separately, replace as needed and reassemble. Then, with a dollop of luck, you should be back motoring.

This is a problem that can be expressed quite easily, and where the boundaries of what is going on are very clear: engine not working, car needs to be driven. Take it apart, analyse, sort out where necessary and reassemble.

But a lot of the time situations are not so cut and dried in life. Where interpretation, information blocks, unconscious motives, organic (rather than linear) development and fuzzy boundaries are involved, traditional IQ will be limited in its ability to assess situations. So when your car isn't repaired on time because the mechanics have two bosses and they are not sure who to answer to, morale is low in the garage and no one is quite sure who takes responsibility for what, and staff have no sense of playing any role in customer satisfaction, another sort of intelligence will be required. It will be the sort of intelligence that asks appropriate questions, generates lots of possibilities and comes up with flexible and inventive solutions. I'm sure I don't need to tell you that this involves creativity. And these fuzzy situations are on the increase, the more complex the world becomes that we live in.

The great majority of us will be familiar with the definition of intelligence as it is tested in school. This is the ability to memorize, analyse and reason verbally. It is splitting things into their component parts to better understand them. It does not involve the emotions or imagination in any way; it derives entirely from an 'I think, therefore I am' concept. This is the basis for a traditional IQ examination, which is often tested through multiple-choice questions with a 'right' answer – a tick-the-right-box approach. It is based on analysis, often ignoring context. Concerns about cultural influences biasing success towards certain groups in these tests have resulted in 'IQ testing' falling out of favour these days, but it is what many tests for 'scholastic achievement' still measure.

The GMAT (Graduate Management Admission Test) is an admissions test used by 2,000 business schools globally, which you can read about at *www.mba.com*. It describes a three-section test that deals with analytical writing, and involves analysis of an issue and an argument; a quantitative section, composed of 37 multiple-choice questions about figures; and a verbal section comprising 41 multiple-choice questions on reading comprehension, critical reasoning and sentence correction. The description of the test is prefaced by an announcement of what it is does NOT measure. This announcement

includes items like knowledge of business and subjective qualities like motivation, creativity and interpersonal skills. We can
only hope that some of the 2,000 business schools that use this
test include other ways of discovering: a) whether students have
some idea of what business is like before they embark on a
career in it, and b) to what extent individual students are motivated, creative and able to relate to others. This is necessary
because, in the real world, interest in business, motivation,
creativity and interpersonal skills are likely to be highly significant determinants of business success.

Writer and professor Henry Mintzberg was interviewed by
London's *Observer* newspaper for his views on the content of
MBA (Master of Business Administration) programmes. He
said the following.

> *MBA programmes concentrate entirely on analytical skills.
> The people who come out of them aren't very imagina-
> tive – they're pretend artists, pretend visionaries, and
> often their grand strategies don't actually amount to very
> much, as we are now finding out in places like AOL and
> Time Warner and Vivendi.*

Traditional IQ tests encourage belief in and orientation to
'one right answer'. As many teachers of creativity in all contexts
will testify, this can condition students in a very unhelpful way.
It will hamper belief in their own self-expression and explor-
ation of possibility. Much of the first year of graduate courses
in art, design and creative writing can be taken up with undoing
the influence of the 'one right answer', and getting students to
create work that is neither right or wrong but just 'is'. The
creative and productive rarely accept that there is only 'one right
answer' and are always looking for alternative possibilities.

The Trouble with Traditional IQ

This definition of intelligence is an extremely limited one, and one that is inappropriate for an understanding of the human brain, which includes much unconscious activity. Memory for instance, seems to work through neurons chatting back and forth across unconscious and conscious thinking. Multiple-choice questions are over-simplistic in the context of a lot of what happens in real life, where it is often far more useful to be thinking 'Who is asking this question and why are they asking it?' Context matters too. It is often very helpful to ask, 'Why is it important to answer this question now in this context?' Of course there are pay-offs to rushing in with a traditional IQ. The 'one right answer to the situation' approach can be quick and help maintain an illusion of power and control. Very important to some of us!

Davina is at a turning-point in her career. She feels that she has got as far as she can in her current role. Her immediate boss, Geoff, is ensconced in his position and seems unlikely to leave for years. At her appraisal, Geoff suggests she should think about moving sideways in the organisation, moving to another company or retraining to do something different. He offers her a multiple-choice route which, Davina thinks may be motivated by a desire to get rid of her, perceiving her as a threat. He suggests that she make her decision in the next three months. She senses that Geoff finds her troublesome and wants her out of his hair as soon as possible. He wants her to come up with one right answer to his multiple-choice question and go. Davina thinks for herself, though, questioning why Geoff should force this idea upon her and impose a time deadline on it. She decides to hold off making any decision about her career until she sees a promotion opportunity within the organisation . . . oddly enough, not something that Geoff has suggested. She thinks of other possibilities in a creative manner that guide her decisions.

a sleeping giant

Studies have shown that high scores on traditional IQ tests, meaning memory, analysis and verbal skills, do not mean that people succeed in life. In large-scale group research, as common sense might predict, people with the top jobs in society tend to have higher IQ levels, while people with the least desirable jobs have lower levels. But George Vaillant's thirty-year study of top Harvard graduates showed that those with the highest IQ were not particularly successful. They did not report higher levels of life satisfaction, either. The graduates that seemed to be the most successful and satisfied were the ones who had long, happy relationships and meaningful work. Freud may have had one right answer when he said the two most important things in life were love and work.

You may have known a school swot who seemed to demonstrate vast reserves of traditional intelligence who was not always successful later on in life. Once out of the educational system, the swot may never have learnt to originate ideas and make them happen. She or he may never have developed their creativity. And people can be highly creative, geniuses even, but not do especially well at school and further education. Charles Darwin, author of 'The Origin of the Species' and originator of the theory of evolution, was described by his headmaster Dr Butler as 'a stupid fellow, who will attend to his gases and his rubbish'. Never mind that 'his gases and his rubbish' changed our entire understanding of what it means to be human. Craig Ventor, initiator of the human genome project, is another, more recent, example of a gifted person who did not do especially well at school.

You need some traditional intelligence to get brilliant ideas and to make them happen. Analysing your market place, what could go wrong, what criticism is useful and what is destructive are all helpful activities. But traditional intelligence limits itself to what currently exists, and that doesn't make for great ideas, which involve speculating about 'what might be'. Like many people, you may believe that you have less potential than you do, because you have not demonstrated high levels of this traditional, analytical intelligence. Several experts concur that it contributes only 20% of influence towards what help people succeed in life. In the next chapter, I help you revisit your beliefs about intelligence. But for now, I suggest that an important form of intelligence exists, which has been overlooked:

Creative Intelligence

I realised, through my research, that very creative people were using their intelligence in a specific way. They seemed to be able to allow their unconscious minds to simmer subjects on a back burner, until their ideas were 'cooked' and ready for consumption. Distinct from traditional intelligence, they used their thinking to put things together in unexpected combinations and unusual ways. They were using synthesis far more than is assessed by traditional IQ tests. They were able to recognise what was new and make sure that other people regarded it in the same manner. When Madonna performed one of her several reinventions with her 'Ray of Light' album, for instance, she successfully combined techno scene, dance music and Asian influences, to produce something new and exciting alongside irreverence and Hollywood glamour. In London, for another example, you can see the London Eye, a creative synthesis between a fairground Ferris wheel, and a high-rise sight-seeing platform. Travelling around the streets of the city, you might come across the London Fashion Bus, a double-decker packed with designer clothes and changing rooms, which visits different parts of the city on specific days. Again, a good example of synthesis, it creatively combines the idea of an ice-cream van with a designer showroom.

When very creative people talk about their work, they will involve their feelings and their fantasies. This is the core of creative intelligence: that we are clever and inventive through emotional and imaginative expression as well as through the channel of calculated thought. Like all sorts of intelligence, what creative intelligence helps us do is to find patterns in different types of environments. It is always focussed on the future and conjecture. It involves the expression of possibilities, of imagination, of what might be.

But having ideas is not enough. What the truly creatively intelligent do is implement these ideas and bring them to communal judgement in a specific environment. Communal judgement, if you are a business manager, may be your team and your superiors; as an entrepreneur, it may be, directly, your market; if you are a scientist, it may be your peers in the scientific community; if you are an artist, it may be your dealer, and their best customers. Whoever they are, there is a strong practical element here, and one that requires skills of persuading and selling. There is no point in having great ideas if you do not know how to make them happen.

So, to sum up, creative intelligence is:

- A set of skills that utilises, your thoughts, emotions and imagination in specific ways to produce ideas.
- A synthesis of these skills which develop better communication between your unconscious and conscious minds.
- Techniques that help you make ideas happen and communicate them to a specific audience, in an effective manner.

It is about having a creative mindset and the process of using this will make brilliant ideas happen.

The CQ spiral

Well, now, it is all well and good knowing what creative intelligence, or CQ – Creative Quotient – *is*, but this is not the same as knowing *how* to get it. Theories only have relevance when they can be applied practically. For that, you need to work out what the creative process involves *doing*. Words like 'freshness', 'greenhousing' and 'illumination' have been used to describe the creative process and traditionally it has been described as a process of: preparation, incubation, illumination and verification. Big abstract nouns, though, are always open to lots of different interpretations, so I prefer to use verbs, or action words, for a process that needs to be applied practically, if it is to be relevant. After all, we are here to *make* brilliant ideas happen.

Ideally, a book like this describes a stage-by-stage process of how to achieve something over a certain period of time. Unfortunately, being creative and having brilliant ideas do not include a linear, stage-by-stage process. It would all be much easier if they did. Rather it is a cyclical, circular journey, with activities starting at some stages and reappearing again a bit later. I like the idea of the creative process being like a spiral, a coiled spring, or one of those metal toys that children play with on staircases called slinkies. When springs and slinkies become stuck in their movement, it often helps to create a bit of energy through pressure lower down in the metal, to get some momentum going. In the same way, in the creative process, when we get stuck, it usually helps to revisit some earlier activities and build up energy there. So, for instance, if you become demoralised after harsh criticism, it would be wise to go back to the first coil in your creative activity and rebuild some belief in yourself.

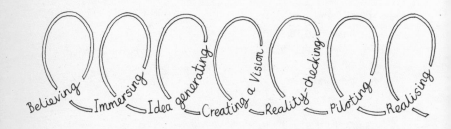

Believing — Immersing — Idea generating — Creating a Vision — Reality-checking — Piloting — Realising

a sleeping giant

The CQ building process consists of:

Believing: Start by looking at your beliefs about your own creativity as well as that of other people. As this book builds your sense of creative know-how, your belief in yourself will increase, which is the underlying theme of this book. As your ideas start to happen, though, you will have to get other people to believe in you and your vision, which is where selling yourself comes in.

Immersing: You can't be half-hearted about making ideas happen; the creative process requires a great commitment from you. This supports you to put in the hours, acquire the skills and mastery, and motivate yourself to create. It is only by throwing yourself deep into the heart of a subject that you can find its essence, play around with different elements and structure and reinvent aspects of it. It means you become saturated in the subject matter which is vital for the next stage.

Idea-generating: You can generate ideas both unconsciously and consciously. Your neurons chatter to one another across these states. You can improve communication between your unconscious and conscious neurons by building CQ, and there are many useful creative thinking techniques available, which means that you can guarantee good ideas, whenever you want them. However, idea-generating depends on how much you immerse yourself in something: to ask questions, you must feel sufficiently engaged and interested in a subject to be intensely curious. Alongside this, ideas need to incubate, to be given time to drift around the mind, and for those unconscious and conscious neurons to hold lots of conversations. If you are operating in a vacuum of any kind, then it will be difficult to generate ideas. Where nothing good is coming into your creativity machine, how can anything good come out?

Creating a vision: When you are clear about your beliefs, totally immersed in your subject and generating lots of ideas about it, creating a vision should come to you very easily, unless, of course, you have got into the habit of seeing yourself as merely a problem-solver. We consider this situation in Chapter Four.

Reality-checking: Once you have a vision, you need to try it out on other people. You must reality-check to improve, of course. This is the nasty business of seeking criticism. We confront this in the next section of this book. Some of the most creative people in the world never make their ideas happen because of their failure to fully engage with criticism. It can be enormously painful, but also enormously helpful. Reality-checking may take some time, and persistence. Legend has it that Harry Potter was rejected nine times before J.K. Rowling got a contract. In business, getting criticism and responding to it are called market-testing and customer relations.

Piloting: Many ideas fall flat because people talk about them, get feedback, but never act to create anything. The best way to convey any idea to someone else is through, for example, some sort of a sample, a version of the service you will offer as a business, a model of how a new design could work, a plan and sample chapters from your novel. But from your point of view too, as a creator, once you have acted on your idea, you will feel much more commitment to it. This is the only way to find out whether it will work or not. How and when you present your pilot scheme is very important and we shall look at this aspect in subsequent chapters. Piloting leads to more reality-checking and it is when you pilot ideas that you seriously start to sell and improve them.

Realising: This is the stage where you may think: 'I've really done it!' There is a strong probability, though, if you have a relentlessly creative spirit, that you are also immersing yourself once again in new subjects, and generating ideas, as you gear up to go on to your next scheme. Realising your ideas, or rather, making something from them, will inevitably involve team co-operation and a knowledge of how markets work.

Every chapter in this book expands upon the stages of this creative intelligence spiral. When you get stuck anywhere while making your ideas happen, then revisiting these stages and seeing where you might move backwards or forwards should prove very helpful.

The Business of eureka

Your ideas will be judged by the world at large. And while some people regard being creative as something 'arty-farty' and rather unworldly, the world itself is absolutely choc-a-bloc full of examples of creative intelligence in all sorts of contexts. Tuning into these will help sensitise your creative mindset.

I'd like you to imagine you are taking part in a psychological experiment. You have been given extra-sensitive creative intelligence antennae, which respond to stimuli when they encounter evidence of good ideas. You get up in the morning, and you read the paper. Your antennae twitch as you read a particularly original and gripping story. You get in the shower with your favourite I Coloniali shower gel. Your antennae twitch again as you look at the well-designed bottle and smell the evocative fragrance. You dry off and look in your wardrobe. You choose your favourite designer jacket, with those antennae twitching around again. You get on your commuter train, and, to begin with, you gaze at the adverts in your carriage and then involve yourself in the latest Paul Auster novel. Everyone else in the carriage looks quizzically at those frantically twitching antennae sticking out of your head.

Creative intelligence produces ideas that influence our beliefs and thoughts. What is known as the 'creative industries' – that is, TV, radio, newspapers, music and the film video-making businesses, book publishing, and design of all sorts – tell us how the world is. But ideas are not just the currency of the media. When you get to the office with a pounding headache and take ibuprofen in an extremely user-friendly form, you are indebted to the creative intelligence of chemists and drug companies. When you turn on your computer and open Microsoft Word, you are indebted to the creative intelligence of hardware and software engineers, designers, and Bill Gates and his legions. Every time we respond to the good idea of another human being, we are responding to their creative intelligence. Whenever we make sense of the world and become inspired by it, it is due to ideas, our own or other people's. It is creative intelligence – what we want and invent – that makes our culture.

People in the business world often have contradictory desires about creativity. The word 'creativity' – with its implications of chaos, contradicting the status quo and uninhibited behaviour – may be a rather worrying one. The business world tends to prefer the word 'innovation', meaning – creativity, as a means of describing, something of value. But business people know, too, that often the critical factor in making a business succeed is the quantity and quality of ideas generated, and how these ideas help the business adapt to rapid change in the environment and market. Bill Gates views creativity as the single most important quality for a business leader. So businesses need creativity, but they may find it difficult to manage.

We live in what is frequently called the 'knowledge economy', which is service-based and depends on the ownership of knowledge and its application. Increasingly, this economy is based on new ideas, which are transferred into ownership via patent, copyright or trademark. These are called intellectual property, the basic unit of which is creative intelligence. People in business talk about 'joined-up thinking' and 'thinking out of the box', but often this chat is merely tokenistic. Businessmen don't fully understand the psychology of creative intelligence and how to organise the environment so that creative intelligence can thrive. They may not fully understand how group dynamics affect creative intelligence in project-based teams. They may not realise that the type of behaviour that leads to promotion in an organisation and the attitudes demonstrated towards dissenters and eccentrics encourage or deter creative intelligence.

The creative industries I described earlier are thriving. In 2001, the creative industries in Britain generated £112.5 billion a year, with export earnings worth £10.3 billion. Growth between 1997 and 1998 was 16%, 10% more than across the rest of the economy. In his book, *The Creative Economy*, John Howkins describes how, since 1999, the USA's most valuable export business has been copyright. Yes, that's right, Disney makes more money than General Motors.

Other businesses are increasingly looking towards the creative industries for guidance on how to manage creative intelligence. Questions like: 'how do you produce things that are new, but also recognisable and categorisable?' or 'how do you retain highly creative individuals in corporate structures?' or 'how do you balance originality with the need for systemic efficiency?' are important in many sectors. The more people understand creative intelligence and how to make brilliant ideas happen, the easier these questions become to answer.

And for people working in organisations, these questions relate to how valued you feel your individual contribution is to the organisation, the extent to which you are able to exert autonomy in your role, and whether your innovative thinking is constantly subject to too much interference from bean-counters. Needless to say, all these aspects greatly affect our motivation at work.

A Sleeping Giant

In the last chapter of this book, I look in detail at the implications of using the ideas in this book – both for you as an individual and in the world at large. My belief is that many of us have a creativity giant inside us, full of enormous potential, who may be snoozing because we do not have the wherewithal to wake him. By the end of this book, he should certainly be stirring . . .

But for now, I just want to consider how things would change if we believed that everyone was essentially creative. What sort of a world would we live in, if there was greater acknowledgement of our creative core? Well, let's start with education. School children would be regarded primarily as creators, but with varying types of intelligence. Teachers would be regarded as highly creative individuals whose greatest skills lie in working out the particular aptitudes of children and nurturing them appropriately. There would be enough scope in the curriculum for a child who loves making cakes to develop their skills as for a child who loves science. But, most importantly, teachers and children would learn creative intelligence skills in order to learn to use their minds in the best way possible, so that whatever subjects they love, they could apply these techniques to them. The main focus of early education would be to, in a creative manner, encourage children, to love learning. We would be nurturing above all else, curiosity, motivation and resilience.

In this creative utopia, politicians would understand that, while the political psyche is one that is attracted to exercising and maintaining power, many other people are more concerned about making things, and achievement, than power. Our leaders would factor this into the systems they designed, asking the questions: 'how can we create environments where people will want to be highly productive?' and 'how can we marry what we need as a country with how people themselves want to develop and learn?' In deprived areas, rather than providing the poor with endless benefits and subsidies, the question they could ask could be: 'what is needed to encourage people here to create an environment where they can feel hope, learn and trade (legitimately!)? Studying human nature and basic psychology would be compulsory for all politicians before taking office . . .

At work, it would be acknowledged that, for great output to occur, people need good input. Grotty environments, surly bosses and endless unrealistic targets are not what makes people perform their best. Inner sources of motivation – like work being meaningful and exercising choice about how you do things – would be given their rightful significance. In the workplace, a key recruitment question could be: 'what does this person like making best: widgets, balance sheets or great relationships?' Find out what a person likes to create most, and you have a happy career track ahead for them. Another key question could be: how does this person best express their ideas?' – whether through utilising mechanical skills, talking, writing or drawing, working alone or in a group. People would be managed on the assumption that they are innately creative, rather than on the assumption that they need commands and control. Bosses would pay a great deal of attention to how people create best and how they are motivated, not only how profitable and target-achieving the organisation is.

Much is made today of the decline in our standards about almost everything: morality, television, eating fresh cooked food, communication between parents and children, etc. While these are, no doubt, exaggerated to make good stories, many of us, I believe, do experience life as rather fragmentary and full of quick-fixes. I don't believe it is rose-tinted Pollyanna-thinking to assert that viewing ourselves and others as being *essentially* creative will help us experience life in a more purposeful way. I like the belief that we are here to make something good out of life.

STAGE 1

The eureka programme: your creative beliefs

We start the programme by looking at your beliefs about creativity, and encouraging you to heighten your creative orientation. If you want to work through the programme entirely, then you will need to arm yourself with an exercise book and pen or new document in the word-processing part of your PC or laptop. The programme will include many proven, effective techniques used in my workshops. You may enjoy working through it with a colleague, friend or relation.

1. Consider what you think about your own creativity. What you believe about your creativity now will affect your creative potential in the future. Take a meander back mentally over your career and education up to the present time. Draw a time line across the page with 0 at the left and whatever age you are now on the right. Think about the big changes that have occurred over that time span and mark them on the line. View these changes as 'defining moments' in your life, where things were never the same afterwards. Remember, though, that 'things being never the same afterwards' can apply to your internal life as much as your external circumstances. Many people report that starting their own enterprise or getting a big promotion at work completely changes their internal self-image. They are sometimes shocked to discover both good

and bad qualities that they never realised they possessed before!

How were you creative during these changes? Were there any entirely new things that you brought into being? Did you come up with creative solutions to problems? Can you recall how you thought, felt and imagined at those times? Describe these feelings, through words, pictures or both. While these memories may not be accurate representations of what happened at the time (more about this theme may be found in Chapter Four), they may affect how you view your creative potential in the future. On my workshops, it is not unusual for people who are very obviously creative to find it very difficult to identify instances in the past where they believe they were being creative. Bleak though it may sound, wherever you experience destruction, eventually you are likely to create something new. Many the business person who creates a thriving enterprise out of redundancy, for instance.

2. While we re on this theme, it s worth considering what you believe about other creative people. Can you think of two or three people who you work with, or are friends or family members, who you judge to be very creative? Remember, anyone in any line of endeavour can be creative. You may want to choose someone famous whom you admire. The critical question you should ask yourself here is: what does this person *do* that makes them creative? How do they behave? You will need to use verbs here; adjectives and nouns are of limited use. You want to identify what these people do   that is, how they behave   as a guideline for what you might aspire to do. So, she s very self-critical is a less helpful

description than, 'she constantly criticises what she is doing, working out what is working and what is not'.

3. This is the point, also, where we need to clarify what you would like to get from this programme. In what areas of your life do you want to have brilliant ideas and make them happen? Please be as specific as possible and remember that, if you spread yourself too thinly, you risk diluting your energy and focus. What do you want this programme to bring into your life? Draw or write your answer. You are considerably more likely to achieve your objective if you commit to it on paper. Don't worry if you can't pinpoint what you want yet. Come back to this question after reading the next chapter, when you should feel more focussed.

4. Finally, in this creative orientation stage, I'd like you to see yourself as having highly sensitive creative antennae, as described earlier. When you've a boring lull in a meeting, or you are stuck somewhere on public transport, look around and listen for creative output from others. Look at the way buildings are designed, the aesthetics in shop and restaurant interiors, the inventiveness of some advertisements and listen to the stories people tell one another. You'll be amazed, I suspect, at what this orientation does to brighten up life.

First stage completed, then. You should have a clearer idea, now, of what creativity means to you and how you want to express it. In tuning in to examples of creativity all around you, you will be starting to put yourself into a permanently creative mindset. Let these questions drift through your mind.

a sleeping giant

As they drift, your thoughts may clarify what you believe about your own and other people's creativity, and what you are aiming for. I am asking you to reflect inwardly more than you possibly do normally. I know from our workshops, though, that many people are not as creative as they could be due to the fact that they have not defined for themselves what that word means.

Now we take a look at the fundamentals of creative intelligence: what you know and what you love.

2

What You Know and You Love

Believing — Immersing — Idea generating — Creating a Vision — Reality-checking — Piloting — Realising

This chapter is about immersing.

Do you remember dotcom fever? Bright young things were starting up amazing business ideas all over the place. It was exciting, it was get-rich-quick and, above all, it felt really creative. Just a very small number of those entrepreneurs have gone on to sustain viable businesses like amazon.com and lastminute.com, though. It is a good bet, also, that dotcom survivors learnt an enormous amount about running successful businesses along the way.

Now I don t want to sound middle-aged here, but, while fresh perspectives and energy are vital for creativity, you still have to know your stuff. For a lot of the dotcom pioneers, not knowing their stuff about business was their downfall.

However, a lot of us don t know what stuff we know. We

may hold limiting ideas about our intelligence and our potential to be creative. When we know what we know and love, we build belief in ourselves. This chapter aims to help with this.

The idea of 'self-esteem' is championed in many self-help books. I am never sure exactly what 'self-esteem' means; it seems to be a stable, feel-good state where you are certain of your worth to everyone and everything. Much more useful, in my view, is the idea of self-efficacy or self-belief: the odds that you give yourself for achieving your goals, and how likely you are to pick yourself up, and dust yourself down, when things go wrong.

Self-belief is something you have to possess if you are going to make your ideas happen. It sustains you when you feel isolated and battered by criticism. It keeps you going when envious souls say 'it'll never work'. It anchors you when you start to doubt your own sanity, because others regard your ideas as a heinous attack on the status quo. It gives you confidence that someone, somewhere, is going to find your ideas relevant. Self-belief means you know that you have something constructive and valid to offer, and feel that you have a right, as a human being, to offer it. Unlike the concept of self-esteem – which implies a general feel-good quality in your attitude yourself towards – you may, despite being insecure and neurotic in some areas of your life, be sustained by the sense of purpose that self-belief gives you. Your friends may say you have something of the Woody Allen about you. Your goals and vision of what you may achieve in your chosen area override any fear of failure and risk of loss of face that you might experience.

As we shall investigate in this chapter, the best way of building self-belief is through immersing yourself totally in subjects that interest you. We are talking full-on engagement here, which is, without doubt, one of the secrets of a satisfying life. It is through this full-on engagement that we understand what it is we know and can speak authoritatively about, and what we love enough to speak with passion about.

What You Know

Footballer David Beckham is sometimes criticised in the press for his lack of articulacy, but here is a description of him by a computer boffin in *The Times* newspaper:

> *Beckham can carry out a multi-variable physics calculation in his head to compute the exact kick trajectory required, and then execute it perfectly. His brain must be computing some very detailed trajectory calculations in a few seconds purely from instinct and practice. Our computers take a few hours to do the same thing.*

When Beckham gets the 'optimal turbulent-laminar transition trajectory' that is impossible for goalkeepers to save – in other words, when he scores a goal – he is using a form of intelligence. Almost certainly this is not traditional IQ, as tested by schools. This football god failed his GCSEs and left Chingford High School at sixteen. These 'detailed trajectory calculations' will be happening in his unconscious mind. Meanwhile, his conscious mind gives little appearance that all of this is going on.

David Beckham then, like other distinguished sportsmen and women, demonstrates very high levels of 'spatial intelligence' and 'bodily kinaesthetic intelligence', two forms of intelligence identified by psychologist Howard Gardener. In his study of highly creative people like Picasso, Einstein, Freud, TS Eliot and Martha Graham, Gardener distinguishes between creativity that is just for oneself, and that which ranges across a broader field. There is a difference here between whether you are having ideas in order to express yourself and feel better, or whether you want to make a great impact on the world through your ideas and make your living out of them. Certainly activities like creative writing have therapeutic benefit. In writing down ideas, people often find it helps them make sense of things. But if you want to make a broader impact with your ideas, then how you communicate them to your field of influence, and your understanding of that field, will be important.

In his book *Frames Of Mind*, Gardener proposes that seven separate human intelligences exist, and focuses on different subject areas as follows.

Words: the ability to use spoken and written words is linguistic intelligence and where we could expect that people like Tony Blair, Bill Clinton, and novelists like Margaret Atwood and J.M. Coetzee excel. This is an aspect of what is considered 'traditional intelligence' and, when you love discussion and persuasion, acting and writing, you'll have it.

Logic and Maths: the ability to analyse problems logically, carry out mathematical calculations and investigate things scientifically. Einstein and Bill Gates would score high here. These two subject areas are what the school curriculum focuses on. So this is another aspect of traditional intelligence, and all you lawyers, accountants, scientists and analysts will possess it.

Music: this is self-explanatory and, though people often speak of musical 'talent', Gardener points out that there are many similarities in the importance of structure in both linguistic and musical intelligence. Just because someone has a lot of musical intelligence, they need not use it, but innovators like Beethoven and the Beatles did. If you've always wanted to sing or play an instrument, but never had the opportunity, then this intelligence may be lying dormant within you.

Bodies: bodily-kinaesthetic intelligence is about the ability to use the whole body, or parts of it, to solve problems, achieve targets and make things. Dancers, sportspeople, painters and surgeons would be people who use this form of intelligence regularly. If you practise massage, cooking, DIY, or any sort of exercise, then you will be using this.

Space: spatial intelligence is the ability to recognise and change patterns of space. This is a useful skill for pilots and navigators, but also for architects, sculptors and map makers. Einstein would have possessed a lot of this kind of intelligence, along with his more predictable logical-mathematical intelligence. Playing Spot-the-ball or obsessing about the furniture arrangement in your home are both instances of engaging spatial intelligence.

Relationships: interpersonal intelligence is part of what today is often called emotional intelligence. It is about understanding what other people want and need, and having the ability to communicate effectively as a result. Bill Clinton, Martin Luther King and Judi Dench would all score high on this one, I imagine. With lots of this, you would be likely to find counselling and group discussion attractive.

Yourself: intrapersonal intelligence means self-knowledge, including understanding what you want, need and fear, and what your resources and limitations are. Self-help junkies everywhere can admit to this one.

More recently Gardener has added two more intelligences to his list – *naturalist intelligence* such as that demonstrated by Darwin and David Attenborough, with an intense understanding of aspects of the natural world, and *existentialist intelligence*: a concern with 'ultimate' issues with a spiritual, meaning-of-life dimension (presumably someone like the Dalai Lama would have a lot of this).

I've just described a mind-boggling range of intelligences. Indeed, you may be starting to think 'is there anything that *can't* be described as a kind of intelligence?' You'll notice there's no sexual intelligence mentioned, though – now *that* could make a good book title! But, considerable though this list is, these ideas go a long way to explaining why the people who generally do best in life are not the school swots. And, funnily enough, we tend to be intelligent in the subject areas we like best. Very creative people tend to be demonstrably gifted in one or two of these intelligences. In business, you are likely to find linguistic, logical-mathematical and interpersonal intelligences dominating.

Creating and Learning

Yuck, for some of us, just that word 'learn' is enough to put us off. It feels earnest, joyless and demanding of effort. But our creative ability is inextricably linked to how we learn. Creativity and learning differ in that creativity focuses on output while learning involves input. But we have to learn and get input in order to create output. Some people think that learning is all about books, but of course, there are many ways of learning. We learn through experience and doing, through requesting and receiving feedback, through talking and through reflecting, quietly, alone. Some people limit their creativity by failing to fully understand all the different ways they can learn. Just going into a strange environment and reflecting on your experience afterwards, or meeting a new person and hearing their story, are less traditional ways of learning.

So what happens when someone believes they 'know it all'? Well, usually, some loss of face has made the person very defensive about learning, and so, in order to protect themselves from the slightest risk of appearing vulnerable, the person defends themselves by trying to project their expertise, above all else. They forget that, to date, no gods have been discovered on earth. The trouble also is that, in doing this, they stop themselves from really seeing what changes are happening around them and how they need to adapt to it. For that is what learning is: adaptation. But, enough ideas – let's get cracking on some practice:

STAGE 2

The eureka programme: what you know

If you don't know already, then you should establish the subject area in which you really want to immerse yourself. What you choose will depend on your individual mind. In what area are you most intelligent?

1. Score yourself between 1 to 10 on each of the following questions:

> • How much do you like talking and/or writing?
> • What about reasoning, working out pros and cons, calculations? (Machiavelli may be your hero)
> • To what degree do you love music?
> • How physically demanding is what you love doing best?
> • To what extent do you like to create patterns in space?
> • Are you a people-person – someone interested in relationships and psychology?
> • To what extent would you describe yourself as self-aware?

I would suggest that you have no qualms about asking a friend or relation if the last question, particularly, proves difficult to score. Because so much of what we do is unconscious, other people may sometimes know us better than we know ourselves. These questions correlate with the seven intelligences described above, and obviously the higher your score on a question, the more likely you are to use that intelligence, and that it will be what you know about. This is the area in which you will want to immerse yourself, where you have the best chance of coming up with brilliant ideas.

Here's an example of someone whose role did not suit their intelligence:

Simon was a solicitor in a large city law firm and unhappy in life. He joined a workshop and rather surprised everyone there when he told us about his profession. His behaviour and dress were very flamboyant. He was extremely warm and funny. When we discussed different types of intelligences, Simon said that he felt he had enough logical-mathematical intelligence to practice law, but actually what he really loved was using interpersonal intelligence. He enjoyed meeting lots of people and dealing with their problems. Clearly, where he was working was not suited to this orientation, with the job's emphasis on long, involved, commercial cases. Seven months later, Simon set up a small practice with one partner, doing lots of legal aid work in the Earl's Court area of London. Today his practice is thriving and Simon can dress exactly as he likes when he goes to work.

Are your circumstances favourable to your being creative by using your preferred intelligences? If not, what can you do about it? How can you restructure your life in order to do something about it?

2. Write your autobiography on, at most, two sides of a piece of paper. Review it by looking at the big

changes in your life, and reflect on how your perspective changed afterwards. These will have been intense learning periods for you, so what did you learn more about? The subjects you learnt most about – people, the need for planning, how useful the exercise could be, etc. – will tell you which intelligence matters most to you.

3. Creativity involves looking at subjects from all angles, and I would like to mention one more perspective on what you know and how you learn. The American Professor Robert Sternberg has researched and written extensively about intelligence, creativity and learning. He describes four different functions of intelligence:

Retaining: this will be the ability to memorise and reproduce key points and definitions. Have you a brilliant track record at exams? Then you will be good at this function. People are, of course, much better at retaining information that is interesting and relevant to them. Memories can be trained through working with ideas in books and on courses.

Analysing: as described in the last chapter, this is in the section on traditional intelligence. Good at academic essays? Then you probably had a lot of this as you compared and contrasted different theories and ideas. Most formal study, even if it is only a part-time evening class, should improve this ability.

Applying practically: this is linking ideas and theories to practical examples – what I am trying to do in the eureka programme sections of this book.

Creating: generating your own theories and ideas – what much of this book is about.

Choose a subject that you believe you know quite a lot about. This can be as mundane as your favourite soap opera or a sports team you support. Now ask yourself the following questions about this subject:

- After a period of allowing the subject to absorb your attention, do you remember a great deal about it?
- Do you like to engage in analysis about it, either reflectively by yourself, or through talking to others?
- Are you keen to put your interest to practical uses, or are you happy to remain an armchair theorist?
- Do you like to generate your own theories and ideas about the subject?

When students were assessed on all of these different types of intelligence, there were some interesting findings. Not surprisingly, students again did best in the areas of intelligence that they liked using most. So those who loved memory tests and games scored well on retentive intelligence, while those who preferred being 'hands-on' scored well on practical intelligence. But students who showed high scores on creative and practical intelligence – excluded largely from many educational systems, which are geared to retentive and analytical intelligence – were far more diverse, both in ethnic origins and social and economic backgrounds. Sternberg concluded that students with creative and practical intelligences were being 'iced-out' of educational systems, with the result that much talent was being lost to society.

So . . . retaining, analysing, applying practically and creating: can you rank these in order of what you like doing best? Just because you are not using a particular kind of intelligence doesn't mean that you don't have it. Can you reactivate your interest in your subject matter and find some new creative input through trying a new approach? Get that old football kit out and have a bit of a kick around or draft your own next episode of EastEnders . . .

4. By now you should be able to be quite definite about the sort of intelligence you possess. Before we finish this section, I'd like you to be quite categorical, too, about how you like to learn. Do you prefer to learn from books, software, listening to people, talking to people, or through practical experience and reflecting upon it? Can you extend any of these preferences to try different learning modes? If you've reached this point, and are still feeling 'well, I still don't know much about anything' then I hate to state the obvious but get out there, decide what you fancy and LEARN!!!! James Dyson, in his autobiography, says that you can learn to be an expert in anything in six months, but if his own experience of developing the dual cyclone cleaner is anything to go by, this means total immersion in something, constant experimentation, and improving upon your creation or subject of study all the time.

5. Finally, the type of intelligence you have is likely to steer you to the subjects you love best. But within any subject, there is usually scope for plenty of different types of intelligence contributions. You get accountants in the music business, and sports coaches with wonderful interpersonal skills. Where you've not found a subject that engages you, it is worth asking yourself the question: 'Given no limitations, what would I do?' and then working out what you can do with that aim, given your limitations.

It's a Love Thing

When John Irving, the American novelist, was asked why he continued to write so prolifically after all of his success, he replied, 'The unspoken feeling is love. The reason I can work so hard at my writing is that it's not work for me'. Creative intelligence involves love in action.

To make an idea happen, you have to really, really want to see it exist. You have to, if you like, love your idea into existence. We know this, I think, when we use words like 'passion' 'wholeheartedness' and 'commitment'. We know these feelings get people through all sorts of obstacles in order to realise their ideas. We appreciate these feelings motivate people for the long haul. Steven Pinker says 'all geniuses are wonks', meaning nerds, and he's right. It is being a wonk and spending so much time, attention and hard work on a subject that produces great insights. We need time to be creative: to try things out and tinker, to look for alternative ways of doing things and other possible explanations. We need to take time to allow ourselves the possibility of stopping and looking at aspects of our field of endeavour in a way that few have done previously. James Dyson, for example, invented a new vacuum cleaner through being obsessed by vacuum cleaners and their shortcomings. Alexander Fleming, the chemist, discovered penicillin through musing about the qualities of mould that he had accidentally grown on a culture. He paused and took time to investigate what had happened in a manner different from the way he had before.

Great creators love what they do, so that they work harder and are more productive than the rest of us. They have generated more ideas, produced more things and maximised the chances of those things gaining acclaim. As Vidal Sassoon, hairdressing supremo, once commented, 'The only place where success comes before work is in a dictionary.' And the founder of IBM Thomas Watson used to advise, 'If you want to succeed, double your failure rate.' When you really love a subject, you want to know everything about it and that enables you to understand the structures, rules and principles inherent in the subject. Like Picasso, who painted astounding classical paintings before going cubist, once you know these rules, you are then able to break them, and create and innovate.

Total Immersion

Now I was brought up in the Baptist faith, and while this can give you any number of hang-ups, like puritanism, workaholicism and excessive deference to authority based on the idea that God is rather fierce, it also introduces its followers, at an early age, to the idea of total immersion. Baptists build deep pools in their chapels where the ministers baptise their followers through total immersion, while the rest of the congregation sing 'Alleluia'. Baptism seemed to me to be a spooky ritual, but the idea of total immersion a compelling one.

Like Baptists, very creative people show that they have more than just love for their area of specialization, by totally immersing themselves in it. They wholeheartedly pursue their interest, sometimes even to the detriment of their relationships, health and personal hygiene. Such people may not be easy to live with. Archimedes himself, apparently, often forgot to eat and to dress. Isaac Newton, Charles Dickens and Picasso all experienced difficulties in their personal relationships. Coco Chanel, who revolutionised the way women dressed last century, commented 'the moment I had to choose between the man I loved and my dresses, I chose the dresses'. While you might not want success at the expense of nourishment, decency and personal relationships, making brilliant ideas happen is not about a dipping your toe in, or having a tentative paddle. It is about a plunge deep into the pool of the subject matter, where you are surrounded completely by content. Some of us find it difficult to dive in with this degree of commitment and abandon.

When people have problems engaging with interests, it is usually because they have been committed and wholehearted about something in the past, and have been punished for it. We see this in relationships, in the person who has their heart broken once, and never learns to trust again. We see it at work when a person has their trust in an employer exploited and becomes cynical, generally, about management. As children we may have been fascinated by something, and wanted to learn a great deal about it, and then experienced shame and humiliation as our learning did not go the way other people thought it should. But that was then, and this is now, as psychologists like to say.

Why is total immersion so helpful? Well, because it is the key to *motivation*.

When we throw ourselves into an activity and involve ourselves in it intensely, we often produce the state known as flow. Described in detail by Mihaly Csikszentmihalyi in the book of the same name, *Flow*, here is his definition:

> *A sense that one's skills are adequate to cope with the challenges at hand, in a goal-directed rule-bound action system that provides clear clues as to how well one is performing. Concentration is so intense that there is not attention left over to think about anything irrelevant, or to worry about problems. Self-consciousness disappears, and the sense of time becomes distorted. An activity that produces such experiences is so gratifying that people are willing to do it for its own sake, with little concern for what they will get out of it, even when it is difficult or dangerous.*

Flow creates optimum performance. When we see a top

footballer run up to take a penalty, moving in perfect rhythm, with his mind and body in complete harmony, we are witnessing him in flow. We often know before his boot strikes the ball that he will score, because his concentration and rhythm are so focussed. The rest of us may experience flow when we are cooking, doing the garden, reading a balance sheet (yes, I know, hard to believe, but some accountants have told me this is the case) or e-mailing our closest friends.

Flow motivates us. What we are doing feels utterly meaningful. We feel we are choosing to do it, and a sense that we are performing well and making progress.

Unfortunately, the way the world is represented to us via the media, flow doesn't get much of a look in. Were we to judge human nature by what we see in films and TV dramas, we would see that people are motivated by money, sex, greed, power and revenge. In these contexts, you rarely see people being motivated by loving something they do, and doing it well. It just doesn't have the same dramatic potential.

But when we reality-check, we see that, for many people, motivators like money and celebrity tend to be short-lived and are ultimately unsatisfactory. Many people who have more than enough money to live on for the rest of their lives keep working because they love what they do, and presumably experience lots of flow while doing it. Why else are Oprah Winfrey, Michael Dell and Paul McCartney – to name but three – still out there and grooving? When you experience flow, you do what you do for the love of the activity itself.

Money and fame are extrinsic motivators: goals that people reach for that are outside themselves. Intrinsic motivation, arising from internal goals and satisfaction, is sustaining and less susceptible to changes. It is more likely to keep you going through changes in external circumstances, like job redundancy, or a change in market taste. We experience the strongest intrinsic motivation by our activity being meaningful for us, by choosing *how* we achieve our goals in the activity and by getting a sense of performance and progress from it. This is the way to achieve flow.

Finding Your Love Thing

Now, finding out what we love in life can be quite difficult. In an ideal childhood world, parents, nursery staff and teachers would observe little you repeatedly trying to operate on Barbie, or applying make-up to Action Man and would note your love of mechanical understanding or cosmetology. They would try and replicate your fascination elsewhere, with a 'look how you can take this book apart' or 'look how you can improve the cover of this book'. But unfortunately real life isn't like that, and little you is far more likely to hear the reprimand, 'Leave Barbie alone; are you trying to ruin her?' or 'Don't put make-up on him; he's a man!'

The good news is that it is never too late to find out what you love doing in life. At the time of writing, UK newspapers are carrying the story of 55-year-old Sheila Quigley, a grand-mother of eight, living in a condemned council house in north-east England, who has just received a £300,000 advance for her first book, entitled *Run for Home*. If you are lucky enough to be reading this book with a clear idea of what you love doing in life, then congratulations. You hold one of the key secrets of a fulfilled life. Where you are less certain, it helps to stop and take stock. And that's what we'll do now.

STAGE 3

The eureka programme: what you love

Throughout this section, you can wear a fake beard, which you stroke a lot, put on some serious spectacles and speak

---

with a strong Viennese accent, if you choose to. That's right – this is the section where you think like a shrink about yourself. There's a lot of asking 'why?'

1. We'll start by establishing where you experience flow. What activity engages you to the extent that you lose track of time, are completely absorbed by it, and feel absolutely satisfied? (Sex aside, that is.) What is it about this activity that you like so much? If it is a leisure activity, compare it with your work activity. What do you love doing best at work and why? People almost always find that there is significant overlap between the reasons why they like specific activities. Below is an example from a workshop of mine.

Sue is the finance director of a big department store. She has made exceptional progress in her career, reaching her position at the age of 27. She doesn't regard herself as the least bit creative. On a workshop, we were investigating what motivated individuals through what they did in their personal lives. To everyone's amazement, the conservatively dressed Sue announced that she had a secret passion: disco dancing. Most weekends, she was to be found boogieing the night away in the town's top nightspots. She loved the glamour and glitz of it all. When we talked about what motivated her at work, she revealed that she found retailing very glamorous. To her mind, parts of the store dazzled and seduced customers. She liked the way that staff were encouraged to put the best of themselves forward to customer – just like disco dancers. She regarded a successful sale between seller and customer as a satisfying exchange in the way that two people enjoy a great dance together. She found retailing sexy and exciting and she tended to emphasize the enjoyment and communication that exists between people. Not surprisingly, Sue saw her role as making this enjoyment possible, and she was the very best sort of creative finance director.

Other typical parallels people draw between what they love in their work and leisure times are: 'being autonomous and needing to deal with the unpredictable', 'dealing with the needs of different parts of the business and pulling them together and getting my family to be happy as individuals and as a whole unit', 'being creative in the garden and creative with the work newsletter' and 'coaching people and seeing them develop – nurturing my family and friends, through food and fun'.

2. How do other people view you and your passions? The other day, I was trying to help a friend of mine find her direction in life. She absolutely refused to imagine possibilities for her future. So we could only investigate the present. She took a blank sheet of paper and then drew herself in the middle of it. Around the stick picture of herself, she drew suggestions and opportunities she had been offered in the past six months. She asked herself 'why did people make these particular suggestions or offers?' It emerged very quickly that what other people were prizing in her was a forensic attention to detail, thoughtfulness and ability to be diplomatic in complex situations. They saw her as being, above all else, thorough, attentive and sensitive. You may find a similar exercise helpful, putting yourself in the middle of a blank sheet of paper, with opportunities that people have offered you dotted about, and then

analyzing what they say about you. Any comments about being a babe or top totty need to be regarded as morale-boosting but irrelevant.

3. Still finding it difficult to identify what you love? Then perhaps you need to put yourself in a different environment to refresh that self-image of yours. You need to ensure that you are getting sufficient stimulation by experiencing different people's worlds. On the ITV show 'Get A Life', where I help people who have got stuck in a rut, career or relationship-wise, the key experience that changes people's lives is putting them into different environments, which shocks them out of their lassitude. Going into different environments can help you clarify what you don't want as much as what you do want. Ask different people if you can visit where they work, or even shadow them for a day. Most people will be flattered by your level of interest and the experience may be a revelation for you. I have done this twice and it was absolutely fascinating. It also stopped me from going into academia, which would have been a disastrous career move for me.

4. Ask yourself some useful questions. When you go into a bookshop, what are you immediately drawn to? Is it travel, which reveals an adventurous spirit, or cookery, which indicates a practical and sensual one? Do your prefer the demands of literary fiction to the escapism of a summer romance? Your book preferences will reflect what you love.

5. This is where the really vigorous beard-stroking needs to occur, as you analyse your own fantasies. When you day-dream, what happens in your favourite fantasies? Are you making stacks of cash, having

your expert opinion sought by important individuals or talking about your amazing ideas to large audiences? What do these day-dreams represent that is really important to you?

6. And on a more slightly more serious note, if you were given the news that you just had six months left on this planet, what would you have regrets about not doing? George Clooney or Kylie aside, what does this tell you about your other passions?

So we started our creative intelligence trail by establishing your beliefs and in this chapter we have gone on to build on your self-belief through identifying and clarifying what you know and love, enabling you to immerse yourself totally in your preferred subject. You finish this chapter, I hope, knowing what subject area in which you want to make your brilliant ideas happen. If not, what the heck, abandon this book immediately and take yourself off on a wild adventure. Meanwhile, the rest of us will take off on a different adventure: a journey into our unconscious minds, vast reservoirs for building creative intelligence. Here we start idea-generating.

3

Your Unconscious Scanner

Believing — Immersing — Idea generating — Creating a Vision — Reality-checking — Piloting — Realising

This chapter is about idea-generating.

It is 1990. Joanne Rowling is travelling from Manchester to London, after a weekend of unsuccessful flat-hunting in the northern city. Not unusually for a train journey in the UK, her train gets stuck for forty minutes in the same spot. She gazes out of the window, day-dreaming. An idea of a train transporting a boy to a school for wizards comes into her mind:

> *All of a sudden the idea for Harry just appeared in my mind's eye. I can't tell you why or what triggered it. But I saw the idea of Harry and the wizard school very plainly. I suddenly had this basic idea of a boy who didn't know who he was, who didn't know he was a wizard until he got his invitation to wizard school. I have never been so excited by an idea.*

And the rest, as they say, is publishing history . . .

It is 1865. A scientist called Friedrick Kekule discovers the structure of benzene. The structure is ring-like, a closed chain, and Kekule makes the discovery after a dream, in which he sees a snake biting its own tail. He later tells the Royal Society: 'Gentlemen, let us learn to dream. But before we publish our dreams, let us put them to the test of waking reason'.

It is 1797. The poet Samuel Taylor Coleridge is feeling 'indisposed' so he takes some opium, a habit he grew rather fond of. Reading a history book about Kubla Khan building a palace, he dozes off. Three hours later, he wakes to find he has dreamt his most celebrated poem. Immediately he starts to write:

> *In Xanadu did Kubla Khan*
> *A stately pleasure-dome decree:*
> *Where Alph, the sacred river, ran*
> *Through caverns measureless to man*
> *Down to a sunless sea.*

Like J.K. Rowling, Kekule and Coleridge, I expect you can identify instances where an idea has popped into your head and you've thought 'well where on earth did that come from?' In this chapter, we investigate where exactly that idea could have come from, and how you can create ideal circumstances for those ideas to come forth and multiply. Here we deal with the essence of eureka moments, those flashes of inspiration and insight that creators and innovators are so fond of describing. So this chapter is about how to make friends with your unconscious mind, and influence it.

But how can we influence something that by its very definition is unconscious? Well, by understanding how unconscious works – and some of this is inevitably speculative – and then consciously placing ourselves in circumstances that make eureka moments possible.

This has been the most exciting chapter in this book to write, and I hope you find it correspondingly exciting to read. In the past ten years or so, there have been enormous advances in what we know about the brain and how it works. Even though there is still a great deal left to be discovered, these advances have led the eminent neuroscientist Antonio Damasio, to conclude that the findings of the past ten years are as great as the whole previous history of progress in psychology and neuroscience. Ideas from evolutionary theory, neuroscience and cognitive psychology are coming together to provide us with remarkable insights into the human mind. Most experts agree that this research is at a very early stage and there is still a vast amount to discover.

Of all the chapters in this book, this is the one that is likely to be the most significant in building creative intelligence in you, a permanent change in how you see the world. When we understand some of the power of the unconscious, we begin to understand the world very differently.

The Unconscious Scanner

It has been estimated that 5%, that is, one-twentieth, of what is going on inside our brains is conscious. This is quite scary, when you think about it. You may have just met someone you find utterly irresistible, and are trying to hold a civilised conversation with them, and just 5% of what is going on is under your conscious control. What is happening between their unconscious and your unconscious? Are you giving the game away? Is your unconscious friend or foe in these circumstances?

This interaction is likely to get you more worried if you accept the Freudian version of your unconscious. Just to remind you, Freud, viewed the unconscious as a kind of container that represses our desires for sex and aggression, and puts us under a lot of pressure in doing so. Today's version sees the unconscious sees as something rather different, something that evolution created to help us deal with complex and unpredictable environments, which probably existed before our thinking became conscious. This is often described as the 'adaptive unconscious', emphasising its evolutionary function in helping us cope with changing circumstances. Psychologists these days tend to view the unconscious as a kind of scanner which combs the settings we find ourselves in for signs of danger.

At the same time that you are reading this book, you are being bombarded by an awesome number of stimuli: sights, sounds, smells, tastes and kinaesthetic (or feeling) signals. Scientists have reckoned on this incredible number being somewhere near the 11 million mark. Your conscious mind is capable of dealing with about 40 stimuli at any one time, so an extremely large percentage of the 11 million is left unaccounted for. And that's where the unconscious mind comes in. While our brains may choose to ignore quite a lot of the 11 million stimuli, and not engage with them in any way whatsoever, the unconscious mind will be dealing with some number of them between 40 and 11 million! Hardly a precise estimate, I know, but as I mentioned earlier, brain research is still in its infancy.

The adaptive unconscious, then, helps us cope with this stimulation and helps direct our attention where it is needed. It gathers information for us that is out of the reach of our conscious attention, it interprets and evaluates that information and it sets goals for us. Rather than the Freudian notion of unconscious urges repressed under conscious thinking, the unconscious is seen as a collaborator with the conscious mind. One of its main goals is efficiency, helping us function in complex environments.

So what's in this unconscious? It contains basic brain functions like memory, perception and language comprehension, which evolved before conscious thinking. It explains why memories just pop into our minds, why we are susceptible to all sorts of visual delusions, and why we simply understand words without thinking about *how* we understand them. Indeed, if you read this sentence very slowly, trying to think about how you understand what you are reading, you will possibly start to find your reading laboured and self-conscious. Similarly, with talking, if you try and work out how you talk, it becomes difficult to do. You can try the same trick with walking. Consciously try and focus on how you walk and you will start to find it difficult: your unconscious wants you to just let it get on with it.

But this unconscious interprets and infers, too, concerning itself with how you judge people and situations, how you feel in certain situations and how you are motivated. It works almost as a spin doctor does, interpreting the world in a way that makes you feel good, and acting as a psychological defense system. It may make you see things in a way that helps you survive so that you don't have to face some brutal reality. We have probably all experienced situations like the one where one individual in a group makes a snide comment about another, and everyone in the group hears it, apart from the victim, who appears to be quite genuinely struck with selective deafness.

The Creative Storehouse

While the unconscious mind may be a scanner rather than a container, this scanner does have storage facilities – a scanner with PC attached, perhaps. In the previous chapter, I mentioned how learning and creativity are inextricably linked. Like motivation, also described in that chapter, learning can be extrinsic as well as intrinsic. For instance, you can learn through formal classroom style teaching, where you consciously apply yourself to analyze, reason and use your memory, or you can learn through totally surrounding yourself with whatever it is you want to learn. It is a lot like the difference between learning a second language in the classroom and learning your first language when you were very small. Learning when you are older involves a lot more conscious effort than early language acquisition. You learnt – eager parents aside – mostly unconsciously then. Extrinsic learning often requires great effort. You consciously apply yourself to getting the stuff that's on the page into your head. This effort may produce emotions that interfere with your ability to learn effectively. In contrast, intrinsic learning is much easier; what you are steeped in just slips into your being. This is learning through experience, or learning-on-the-job, or enjoying yourself so much while doing something that you do not realize you are learning.

Your unconscious mind holds all sorts of learning and knowledge. A build-up of tacit knowledge resides there, rather than hard facts like how a subject works. It's a kind of accumulated wisdom, I suppose – an idea popular with those of us who are approaching middle age. Our memory neurons usually tag long-term memories with emotional significance, and these may be stored unconsciously, which explains why, when you meet someone who reminds you of that dodgy girl or boy friend you knew ten years ago, you feel intuitively uncomfortable. Rather than consciously thinking 'this person reminds me of that dastardly individual', you simply have an instinctive response to the person, which later on may bring up a conscious reason for it.

Neurons communicate with one another across spaces called synapses. When you learn something new, electrical impulses fly across the synapses, creating new neural pathways as they travel from neuron to neuron. So, learning refreshes and rewires your brain and helps you generate ideas, sparking possible connections not previously made.

Much of what you know about the world and how it works will be stored in your unconscious mind. Your conscious mind does not have sufficient capacity to hold this information; it would crash if it were required to do so. The unconscious is where most brilliant ideas come from – from your experiences, memories and learning – and the better you can access this storehouse, the greater your chances of creative success.

Prove It!

The idea that so much of what goes on in your mind is unconscious can be a threatening one. It makes you feel less powerful than when you believe that much of what you do is under your conscious control. So, quite understandably, a lot of people resist the idea of a powerful unconscious. For the control freaks and sceptics amongst you, here is some proof.

The scary monsters

What do you see here? The effect of unconscious perception on perspective makes most people see a big scary monster chasing a small one. But measure them and you will find that they are both exactly 4.6 cms!

A party trick

You are at a party, engrossed in conversation with two interesting and attractive people. The room is quite crowded and the noise level is quite high. But, from a group about six feet away from you, a name is mentioned, your name. Immediately your ears prick up and you try and hone in on the conversation consciously. But what heard your name in the first place? It was the same volume as the rest of the conversation that group were having, yet somehow it got to your ears . . . could it be from your unconscious scanning the room?

Red alert

It is a hot, dank day. You are walking along a dingle, very shady, where a stagnant river runs at the bottom. You mount some steps to come out of the dingle and, out of the corner of your eye, you see something dark that appears to move. You freeze immediately, on full rat alert. Then, as your conscious mind realises it is not a rat, but an old shoe, you relax. Your unconscious mind had gone into red-alert-rat mode. When your slower conscious thinking worked out what was really going on, you could stop worrying. Joseph le Doux, a neuroscientist, describes how we have two emotional pathways in the brain. The first, which responds quickly and unconsciously to the perceived danger, gets information very fast, with minimal processing, from a sensory part of the brain (the thalamus) to an emotionally responsive part of the brain (the amygdala). The second carries information from the thalamus to the cortex, a part of the brain involved in information processing that makes more informed judgements.

Unconsciously Primed

Dr. Edouard Claparede provided evidence, way back in 1911, of unconscious priming – the process by which the brain sends messages to the unconscious without the conscious mind being aware of it. A female patient of his was unable to have memories because of brain damage. She lived entirely in the present moment, so that, if five minutes elapsed between her first encounter with another person, at the second encounter she would once more greet them as a stranger. Claparede decided to use her condition for an experiment. The next time she came to see him, he hid a pin in the palm of his hand. (The ethics of scientific experiments in 1911 were not as closely monitored as they are these days.) She shook his hand, for, as far as she was concerned, it was her first encounter with him. Upon doing so, she shrieked and recoiled with pain. On her next visit, she showed no sign of wariness as she met him and once more greeted him as though he was a complete stranger. But there was one difference. She would not shake hands with him and, when Claparede asked her why, she could offer no reason. Her unconscious was holding the painful memory, and protecting her.

We can certainly be primed unconsciously to alter our behaviour. When a group of elderly people of similar fitness and mobility were asked to walk a certain distance, those before whom the word 'elderly' was flashed quickly and imperceptibly before them, walked more slowly than those who had not seen it. When customers look at advertisements suggesting excellent service, they will rate those containing a clock on the wall as more effective than those without one – even though they may not be consciously aware that the clock is present. Even estate agents – that hard-bitten bunch of operators – are not immune to this effect. When a group of experienced estate agents was asked to guess the cost of specific properties, and primed beforehand with figures significantly higher than their real prices, they all guessed wrongly and overestimated their true costs. It seems we are so keen to make sense of things that we grasp at any ready markers we are offered.

And Falling Over . . .

It is extraordinary how much of the brain's activity the unconscious part of the mind governs. How do we know how to move our limbs to get out of bed in the morning, for instance? From a sixth sense, of which we are not conscious, called proprioception. In his book, *Strangers to Ourselves*, Timothy Wilson describes what happens when this sense is damaged:

> *The physician Jonathon Cole documented the case of Ian Waterman, a man who suffered nerve damage when he was nineteen and lost all proprioception. Mr Waterman was like the straw man in* The Wizard of Oz, *newly released from his pole. If he tried to stand, he ended up a heap of tangled limbs on the floor. As long as he focussed on his arm or leg he could keep it still, but as soon as he looked away, it would start moving uncontrollably. With a great deal of courage and hard work, Mr Waterman was able to regain some control of his body, by replacing his unconscious proprioception with conscious attention. He learned to walk, to dress himself and even to drive a car by watching himself carefully with fierce concentration. He literally kept an eye on himself at all times, because he was in trouble if he lost sight of his body. One day he was standing in the kitchen and there was a sudden power failure, casting the room into darkness. Mr Waterman immediately fell to the floor. Because he could not see his body, he could no longer control it.*

Chattering Neurons

You can't control your unconscious mind because it is just that: unconscious. But you can use your conscious minds to create circumstances that give you inspiration. Inspiration is just another word for learning, really, in that both provide stimuli for new connections and new ideas.

So is it possible to improve communication between the conscious and unconscious mind? Well, it helps to regard the brain as being full of neural circuitry, including circuits for activities like playing and seeking, which are directly related to creativity. The image of your neurons chattering to one another both within and across circuits is a useful one here. Think about how it feels when memories come to mind. The sensation you have is of something in the present stimulating unconscious experiences stored in your mind from the past. This is like the instance I described earlier, when you meet someone that you respect to strongly, but are unable to consciously identify where that feeling comes from. It is only after the event, when you are relaxing or engrossed in something else, that you suddenly remember who the person reminds you of.

It seems probable, then, that if you are slightly anxious in a situation because of the response a person evokes in you, that the neurons and circuits responding to anxiety might interrupt the conversation between your memory neurons. That is, your reaction interrupts the conversation between the conscious and unconscious memory neurons, making communication difficult.

It's the sort of situation most of us have experienced when someone demands that we come up with a great idea, immediately, and we know there is absolutely no possibility of this happening because of our heightened state of tension. But later on, when the feeling of anxiety has passed and the neurons causing it are silent, then other conscious and unconscious memory neurons are able to resume conversation. Logically, then, the best sort of communication between your conscious and unconscious mind will happen when your attention is focussed in a particular direction: that of reflection.

In order to get the best access you can to experiences and knowledge lodged in your unconscious, you need to develop skills for managing your attention, as far as this is possible. Indeed, creativity aside, in the blitzkrieg of stimulation that most city-dwellers inhabit, this would seem a very necessary day-to-day survival skill.

STAGE 4

The eureka programme: stimulation and drift-time

You can treat your unconscious mind rather like a favourite pet, making sure that, on one hand, it gets enough varied stimulation and, on the other, plenty of time to drift and chill out.

1. Your unconscious mind is particularly sensitive to new information, and one of the core skills that creative people have is sensitivity to what is new. Mindless routine can kill this facility. You don't experience anything new, so your senses become dulled to it. More varied input is better input; just different faces and places will do the trick sometimes. I'm not suggesting you drop everything and go off venturing around the globe but if you feel you are in a rut, then try a different route to work, arrange to catch up with old friends, try a new kind of cuisine or see a great film. Just change your world a little.

2. Give yourself drift-time. There is great social kudos to

be had from being busy constantly, the implication being that others want you – a lot!

We live lives that are based upon hard concepts of time. We work set hours, have specific quality time hours with our children and schedule activities and social events for our leisure time. This kind of time is hard-edged, full of boundaries and deadlines.

If, as I am suggesting, the unconscious has several different timelines: very fast for red-alert processing and much slower and open-ended for contemplation, mulling things over and accumulating wisdom, then 'hard time' may not help in accessing the unconscious. Hard time involves frequent dead-lines, a strict timetable on gaining and a strong focus on gaining rapid results. Soft time involves a much more open-ended view of time, where you feel you have a long period to potter and play. It's the sort of use of time you experience when you have week-ends or days off and think that glorious question 'what shall I do today?' or when you play in an un-focussed way with small children.

So, to develop creative intelligence you need to give yourself 'drift time' periods where you have no immediate deadlines and your conscious neurons are not yelling to all the others 'Go! Go! Go'. Instead, they actually experience silence, and an opportunity to hear what some of the other quieter, slower, more tentative neurons are saying.

On our workshops, Stephan Stockton, my collabo-rator, just gets everyone to turn their chairs away from the centre of the room and drift mentally for a few minutes. It is fascinating how much this changes the mood in the room, and also how helpful people find it.

This may well have occurred to you already, but regular scheduling of drift time, along the lines of 'every Wednesday and Friday between 6 and 8 pm I will schedule drift time' is to miss the point too. This needs to be something that is irregular – not always planned – and varying in length.

Our need for drift time partly explains the great popularity of alternative therapies at the moment. When you are lying on a couch having aromatherapy, Reiki or hot stone massage, you are being openly encouraged to drift – and paying for it too. A cheaper alternative is to try Stephan's technique. Just turn your chair away from whatever you are doing and drift for a few minutes.

3. Try yoga, meditation or Pilates. It is widely believed that reflective practices make people feel better and help with all sorts of conditions. The conscious chatter of neurons is quietened during these disciplines. It is no coincidence that Archimedes had his eureka moment while he was in the bath. There was no better opportunity for productive neuron discussion, and for those unconscious neurons to shove the new pattern they had detected in the direction of the conscious ones.

4. You can get into the habit of reflection by consciously practising it. You will need some soft-time to do this, though; twenty minutes can be enough. If you are not of a reflective disposition, you will probably find it easiest to do this alone, somewhere quiet. You can close your eyes, or look at something calming, like a favourite painting or trees and the sky. It can help to consciously slow down your breathing, but check that it is low in your body, and your stomach distends as

you breathe in. When you are having problems clearing your mind, think of a simple shape like a circle or a square and just focus on that. Once you are feeling sufficiently calm, just turn over a recent disturbing experience or idea in your mind. Keep a part of your mind slightly detached, so that it looks at the experience or idea dispassionately. You may find it helpful to imagine you are seeing it in a completely white setting, from a distance. A part of you just coolly observes it. Then notice how you are responding physically both during the reflection and afterwards. Much of what happens in our bodies is unconscious, and focussing your attention on it can give you real insights. Do you feel more tired, have you tensed up, or did you alter your posture so that you became more upright and upbeat?

Lucy, a research chemist, described this experience thus:

I had been on a workshop where I had what I felt was a helpful insight into a research project I was running at work. But I wasn't sure whether I had just got carried away with the enthusiasm and positive thinking or the workshop, or whether my insight was a generally useful one. So the following day, I just sat for ten minutes and reflected on the workshop and my insight. I noticed that my posture had improved, I felt energetic and purposeful – all good, positive signs, I felt, that the insight was worth acting on. I think it's always helpful to check your conviction before checking what others think.

When you drift off into day-dream, provided you are not driving on the M1 at the time, resist the impulse to jerk yourself back into full consciousness and enjoy your reverie. Again, notice the ideas and images that float across those unconscious and conscious neurons of yours. You are probably giving your mind a well-deserved rest from relentless conscious activity, one that may turn out to be creatively productive.

5. Your unconscious mind may be drifting very productively as you sleep. When you are engrossed in getting an idea off the ground, ask yourself two questions as you sink into sleep: what might be possible here and how could circumstances change? You may wake in the morning having experienced an overnight eureka moment.

What You Really, Really Want

You can use reflection to help you work out whether you are thinking or doing something because it is socially desirable and there is peer group pressure to conform, or because you really want to do it. It can help you sort out whether the goals of your unconscious mind and your conscious mind are aligned or at odds with one another. You can use it to confirm that the ideas you are pursuing are the ones you are really attached to – both consciously and unconsciously.

An experiment looked at a group of people who were engrossed in an activity they liked doing, for a reward. Then the reward was taken away. They were asked to repeat the activity. In all that could be observed, the signs were that they enjoyed the activity as much as, if not more than, before. But, immediately after the experiment, they were all asked which activity they preferred: the one they were rewarded for or the one without reward? They all replied, not surprisingly, the one they were rewarded for. They were then asked to go away and reflect on the two activities and to report back later on whether their feelings had changed. The great majority of them came back and said that, after reflection, they felt they had enjoyed the rewardless activity as much as the rewarded one, for its own intrinsic worth. After reflection, their judgements of their responses were much more in line with what had been observed. Please note, this does not imply that we can survive on job satisfaction alone!

Intuition Ain't Always Right . . .

Intuitive feelings – based on links between conscious neurons experiencing 'now' talking to unconscious neurons from the past – may not always be accurate. Your mind may leap from the great idea you have just come up with to a similar great idea you had five years ago, and the connection between them screaming, 'This will be fantastically successful!', completely forgetting that the world you will be launching your old idea into has changed dramatically in five years. Therefore, intuitions, these leaps between ideas, need checking with external reality. This means asking other people what they think about your intuition, and testing your intuition in different environments: actually going to places where your idea could be implemented, and seeing if it is a viable reality.

Intuition is more likely to be accurate when you have experience in the subject it concerns. Your unconscious mind detects signals based on past experiences; these signals indicate to the part of your brain governing emotions that you should feel a certain way. You may have a lot of experience making business deals, for instance, so that you intuitively know when a new deal will work: unconsciously your brain has picked up on a combination of features in the deal, which it knows to have been effective in the past.

eureka!

Imagination and Memory

Having brilliant ideas is about using your imagination, moving from the 'what actually exists' of analytical thinking to the 'what might be' of creative intelligence. No imagination – no ideas. And memory creates your imagination, providing it with content and assembling experienced notions in various combinations. A lot of this activity will be unconscious. But you can exercise both your memory and your imagination through understanding how they work and building your imagination muscles. As you will see shortly, top athletes develop both their bodily and imagination muscles so that they work together.

To experience this, in your mind's eye, I'd like you to see a big, fat, fragrant lemon. Now I'd like you to see yourself cut this lemon into quarters with a sharp shiny knife, pick up a quarter, and suck it hard. Now, check how your mouth feels; quite probably, you are producing lots of saliva, just as though you had just sucked that lemon.

The power of the imagination is very great. In *How Brains Make Up Their Minds*, the brain scientist Walter Freeman comments: 'all that we can know comes through the imagination, which allows us to generalize and abstract to create the internal structures with which we act and understand'. The currency of the imagination is mental imagery which we can create via the senses – seeing, hearing, tasting, smelling and feeling. Like memory, it seems likely that mental imagery crosses over between unconscious and conscious neurons, and that their ability to communicate with one another is likely to be affected by whatever else is going on inside the brain. Mental imagery is extremely powerful. Sports psychologists at Loughborough University in the UK have demonstrated that athletes can produce 90% of the physical changes that produce peak performance while sitting still visualising themselves reaching that peak performance. All top athletes will train their imaginations as well as their bodies.

Whenever we talk about the future, we use our imaginations. And mental imagery must depend on what is stored in the memory. So when we get scared, for instance, we are using our imaginations in a certain way to predict dire consequences based on past experience. The trouble is, of course, our memories lie. We do not remember things as they actually were, unsettling an idea though that is.

Our memories are subject to all sorts of revision, depending on the mood we are in, and the context and social desirability of their content. You can experiment with this by revisiting a holiday scene in your memory. When most people do this, they see themselves sunbathing on a beach, whizzing down a ski slope or relaxing by a lake. But of course, this isn't how it actually was. What actually happened was you were squinting up at the sun from your striped towel on the beach, or you were aware of white snow and green trees zooming past your sightline or you inhaled the pine-scented, cool lake air.

A researcher called Linda Levine interviewed a group of participants about their feelings over the outcome of the O.J. Simpson trial in 1995. They described happiness, anger or surprise. Five years on, she interviewed them again and asked them to recall how they had felt at that time. Their descriptions were very different, and much more in line with their current levels of happiness, anger or surprise. For the most part, they were unaware that their initial feelings had been different.

This is similar to what happens when people are asked about the early stages of long-term relationships. Where the relationships are happy ones, then the people involved are likely to report ecstatic early encounters. Where the relationships have turned sour, then people are likely to report that the early phases were bumpier than is really true. Hindsight is a marvellous thing.

Although the memory lies, we have to believe that some

memories are stable and accurate. They create our auto-biographies, tell us where we've come from and give us indications as to where we might go in the future. Memory also links our inner and outer worlds. When people lose their memories, they lose the ability to maintain social relationships. Much of what we talk about with one another is an exchange of memories – composed of stories, personal experiences, opinions, etc. – and through this exchange we hope to establish common ground. The Harvard Professor, Gerald Zaltman, says that many of our cultural institutions are repositories for shared memories. Holidays, art, films, literature, myths, schools and universities all hold meaning for us in the form of memory. And of course we associate all of these entities, quite rightly, with enormous creative potential.

Memory stores all sorts of content: instructions on how to do things, tacit knowledge, symbolic associations and stories. You may have heard this description of our learning process, which says that, at the outset, we are unconsciously incompetent, not having identified our shortcomings. Then we become consciously incompetent, aware we are not doing well. Then we become consciously competent, aware that we are improving. And finally, we become unconsciously competent, the new awareness stored in unconscious memory. We initially store memory in a form known as engrams, then, if useful, we move these short-term memories into long-term storage. I've already mentioned that long-term memory becomes tagged with emotion and our senses can recall that emotion. For instance, whenever I smell the aptly named *Je Reviens* perfume by Worth, I am back at my mother's dressing table as a ten-year-old taking a surreptitious squirt from her perfume canister.

Your memory plays a highly significant role in your ability to be creative and have great ideas. It needs to be well-oiled and rather efficient. Here's how to activate those neural connections.

STAGE 5

The eureka programme: forwards and backwards

1. Memories become fixed through repetition, even though they may not be entirely accurate. Several years ago, I witnessed a hit-and-run incident. The police officer at the scene of the crime got me to repeat my statement five times before I was allowed to leave the scene. Two different officers transcribed it. I had the feeling I was being made into a water-tight witness, should the case ever come to court. But when I reflected on it, I was not at all sure that my first account was accurate, even though I certainly remembered it.

   You may have fixed memories that stop you from generating ideas and making them happen. These memories could involve failure, looking silly, feeling personally rejected. Perhaps you came up with an idea once, and someone poured scorn on it publicly. Consciously replay the memory but change the ending; make yourself a dazzling success, a person who shrugs off humiliation with a peal of laughter, or an outcast who goes on to much better and brighter company. Replay this new scenario several times, and make a mental note to yourself that every time your sabotaging memory arises, you will feature the new outcome.

2. 'All great achievements emanate from the unconscious,' says Gene Lambrun, a researcher who has conducted detailed analyses of the lives of great creators. He claims that the two most important influences on great creators are the heroic archetypes they encountered in their childhoods and a desire to

compensate for losses experienced then. Frank Lloyd Wright, for instance, who revolutionised how America and eventually the world viewed architecture, was brought up by his mother with the belief that he was an incarnation of the ancient Celtic god, Taliesin. That is the sort of influence that would be unlikely to see you shelf-stacking in the supermarket. Have you got heroines or heroes in your memories who act as role models for what and how you want to achieve? Are you able to consciously identify what they did that you admire?

And now the compensatory aspect. Many are the individuals whose main quest in life has been to have a stable and happy family life, following a painful divorce between their parents. This is no bad thing, necessarily. Is there something in your memory banks that you are working to put 'right' or to do very differently? A friend who fronts a rock band told me that, during much of his childhood he felt powerless because of his desperately unhappy mother. Then, when he put his first band together, he experienced feelings of power and effectiveness that he became addicted to, and kept on wanting to replicate.

3. Now move your attention to the future. Are you preventing yourself fulfilling your creative potential through creating imaginary disaster scenarios for the future? Again, you may be playing the anti-heroine or hero who fails dismally, looks silly or is mocked and rejected by everyone. Replay these future scenarios with a more realistic, balanced outcome. If you see yourself being pelted with accolades, while it's a nice trip, you could be setting yourself up for disappointment. Instead, imagine people expressing mixed reactions, some perhaps privately liking what you

have done. See yourself maintaining your belief in yourself, while collecting others' reactions as part of your ongoing research.

4. Exercise your memory. When you meet new people, or encounter some information you are keen to retain, give it a visual image and record feelings to store it effectively. Remember people by mental pictures of their enthusiasms, fears or the feelings they evoke in you. Memory experts suggest using locations as a way of training your memory: create pictures of what you want to remember at specific locations in your home, and look at those pictures in the locations. So if you met a chef called Peter, you'd remember him in front of your cooker, wielding a spatula and wearing his chef's hat.

5. Take plenty of exercise and eat oily fish, or take fish oil in order to boost memory performance. You want Omega 3 and Omega 6 anti-oxidants in some form. And scientists have proven that memory produces most recall, overnight. So get plenty of sleep. When you are keen to come up with a new idea, mulling over influences on the idea before you sleep may help that idea appear in the morning.

Stories and Metaphors

As you read this book, you should be developing an increasing sense of how important communication is in making ideas happen. This communication involves neuron chatter, as described in this chapter, and talking about our ideas to others. A core unit of the way that we make sense of the world and communicate that sense to others, is via telling and hearing stories.

For the great majority of us, stories will have been the

earliest education we received. Long before we could talk, our parents and carers told most of us stories. We know this form of communication has beginnings, middles and endings, and is particularly satisfying to listen to. In fact, the memory, unconscious and conscious, holds a lot of content in story form.

Our imaginations will predict stories that could unfold. Some psychologists even think we unconsciously script our lives, without realising it, and then do everything we can to ensure that the script is played out. Certainly when we think of tragic characters like Princess Diana and Paula Yates, this seems a relevant idea: there was no way those two were going to fade into a genteel old age.

Whether you script, unconsciously or not, you will explain your life and those of other people in terms of stories. What you believe to be the culture of the organisation you work for, will be made explicit via stories – of its growth, alliances, starring personalities and good and bad fortunes. A story gets to the heart of a matter; it puts humanity into ideas. The most gripping stories are always reality based, and to some extent must reflect our knowledge and beliefs about the world.

People who regard themselves as highly logical, fact-orientated individuals can have problems viewing themselves as storytellers. But when you ask such people to provide a case history or relevant example to illustrate the point they are making, they do this quite readily. They are, of course, then telling a story. They are also forgetting that every time they open their mouths to speak, they make it up. They are also forgetting that every time they present themselves at an interview, or put forward a case in a meeting or offer a presentation, they are telling a story. The interview kind of story is a selective view of their autobiography, a 'this is my tale so far'. At the meeting or presentation it is 'here is the story of the project so far, and why we need more resources, involvement from you, more time', or whatever it is that you are seeking.

So how do stories help you generate ideas? Well, your unconscious and conscious minds deal in stories. Very often when you want to make sense of something, you spot a few signals that seem relevant, then create a narrative around it. The signal-spotting and narrative may be travelling across those unconscious and conscious neurons again. Both infer meaning. Below is an example of this.

Tony is about to run a workshop for a large group of his employees at work. His wife Anne, who has worked for the company for many years, looks at the list of attendees and comments, 'Oh no, not Eric', and then goes on to describe a noisy, demanding, childish individual. When Tony meets the team, he believes he spots Eric immediately. Focussing on running the workshop, Tony is vaguely aware that Eric seems to be very talkative, and potentially disruptive and unsettled. He becomes more fully conscious of it when Eric asks some difficult questions. When Tony gets home that evening he says to Anne, 'My goodness, you were right about Eric, and compounding it with that dress sense . . . he wore a burgundy jumper with his ginger hair'. 'Ginger hair?' replied Anne, 'But Eric's got black hair . . . and I can't believe he would dye it'! Clearly, Tony had been barking up the wrong Eric all day long.

So, what you infer from what you see may not always be correct and will affect how you receive what is going on around you.

The Harvard psychology professor David McClelland conducted extensive research in India, helping aspiring business people to become more entrepreneurial. One of the most effective methods he found of increasing their awareness and confidence in this was through stories. He first got them to listen to and construct stories about themselves and others being constructively entrepreneurial. Then he got them to listen to inspiring and informative stories about many different entrepreneurs. McClelland's results were impressive and convincing and showed that his students had become more entrepreneurial. So, steeping yourself in the right sort of stories can help you succeed creatively.

When you apply the story form to your ideas, you find out where those ideas are coming from and where they are going. You discover how they fit in with stories other people are creating with their lives. The more you apply the story format to how you develop your ideas, and how you sell them to others, the more effective you are likely to be. Stories give you something we all need, especially when you are listening to tentative, open-ended matters like ideas. Stories give us coherence.

Creativity of any kind emphasises the extent to which human beings share common ground. All cultures tell stories and all cultures use metaphors. Metaphors link two ideas from memory with one another. They compare one world or set of ideas with another, and are produced by the imagination. Metaphors help generate ideas, because they get us to see things differently, and in different contexts, just like Kekule's dream of the snake helping him discover the structure of benzene, cited at the beginning of this chapter. Producing metaphors is yet another brain activity that gets those unconscious and conscious neurons chattering like mad to one another.

The most powerful metaphors are based on universal images, which people from all sorts of different cultures recognise. Snakes, for instance, are universal images, hence their widespread use and significance in myth and ritual. As we might expect, because everyone experiences them and they are all around us, they come from everyday universal like space, notions of time and the human body. We speak of people being 'a pain in the neck' or of 'having to shoulder responsibility'. We read of a 'sickness at the heart of government' or 'spineless attitudes'. But the best metaphor in relation to this chapter, is when we talk of people 'having lost the plot'. We know, unconsciously, that we live our lives as stories, and when someone's life goes haywire we use the obvious metaphor. Going metaphorical is a wonderful way of exercising those neurons in creative cross-talk, and of generating brilliant ideas.

STAGE 6

The eureka programme: story telling and going metaphorical

1. Starting with yourself, work out three different versions of your life story. Stories need clear beginnings with a triggering incident, obstacles that get in the way of where people want to go, conflict and climax, and they need a good strong ending. Without good endings, stories like those of Osama Bin Laden and Saddam Hussein can be very worrying. We like to see baddies get their comeuppance. One of these three versions of your life story should include a role for you as the great creator, in your choice of subject matter. This is an opportunity to check whether, auto-biographically, you have a version of yourself making brilliant ideas happen. If not, get one now, please!

2. You will put yourself onto a 'story footing' if you analyse what you read in the papers and receive on radio and TV, and review them critically as stories. You will see the same themes reappear time after time. 'Politician getting too big for their boots', 'hideous amoral criminal getting away with it', 'local girl/boy/animal makes good' and 'very worrying news about health threats' are just some of the most common ones. Sharpen up your storytelling instincts by making up stories instantly about people you see on the street or public transport, or those who are

---

boring you into a reverie in that dreary accounts meeting. You can make them luridly sexual if you like. No one need ever know. With practice, you can hone up your story-making skills, so that they almost become second nature to you and you can quickly make stories about almost anything that happens. This ability will give you a creative mindset.

3. Creative writing teachers suggest one of the best ways to access the unconscious is through 'early morning pages' – that is, immediately writing as soon as you get up in the morning whatever is in your mind. (Twenty minutes of this should be productive. This may be a suggestion of limited use to those of you who, like me, hear 'Mum Mum, where are you?' every morning upon waking.) The same teachers also suggest revisiting the great classical myths and fairy tales for inspiration – because all of storytelling's great themes and conflicts are there. Getting great ideas may involve putting mythical elements into unexpected settings.

4. Shape your ideas as soon as you can into coherent stories. And then ask yourself what stories will people on the receiving end be using? For instance, will the finance director be using the story of 'wild and whacky idea that will inevitably lose us loads of money?' Where do your ideas fit in with other projects and successes that you or your organisation has been involved in? And for you, personally, how does the story you want to tell, with your new idea, fit in with the rest of your life story and career history? Is it an inevitable outcome story, for instance, or the chance of a Cinderella moment for you, a story of total transformation?

Talk about your ideas in the story format as much as possible. Socially, try to tell a few more stories to get comfortable with the form.

5. Sharpen up your metaphorical powers and start to enjoy boring meetings or train journeys. Go metaphorical in your head about other people. For instance, if you have a moment to kill, ask yourself, 'what is this particular person or experience like, in one word?' Enliven meetings or waiting room experiences by asking yourself 'if that person over there was a container/animal/Hollywood film star/building, who or what would they be?' Doodling, writing stream-of-consciousness style, where you just let the words tumble out on the page without restraint and with wild fantasising, where you see yourself as some siren or god, can all help with going metaphorical. The key question is always: 'what and where are the parallels?' Our choice of metaphors will always reveal unconscious imagery; where you draw work as being like a prison, or home like an alarm clock, you know something needs to change.

6. Use metaphor to think about your ideas, the environment you work in and how you feel. Strong metaphors should help your ideas develop and help you communicate them more effectively to others.

Unconscious Behaviour

The BBC made a film about the relationship between Tony Blair and Gordon Brown. I was lucky enough to be asked to examine lots of old footage of the two of them over the years and to give my views on what it revealed. One of my favourite excerpts was of a Labour Party Conference. Tony Blair was heaping fulsome praise on his chancellor Gordon Brown, who sat, granite-faced, by Tony's side. Then Gordon got some imaginary fluff on his lapel, and, as Tony eulogised about his sidekick, Gordon started to violently and repeatedly flick the imaginary fluff off his jacket, jaw clenched. It was impossible not to conjecture that that imaginary fluff represented Tony's nose . . .

I am sure that, had anyone asked Gordon Brown about his behaviour during Tony's speech, he would have had no conscious recollection of the fluff-flicking incident, as it shall be known. This was his unconscious operating – an unconscious that was saying 'this is uncomfortable for me; I would rather not be experiencing it, and it is making me angry'.

Observing unconscious signals in other people's behaviour is one of the most interesting ways of gaining insight into their true motivation. Research shows that, on the whole, we are not very accurate in assessments of our own motivation. Other people – friends and colleagues – tend to be able to make at least as accurate assessment, if not better.

Where you feel you may have a clash between what you consciously want, and what your unconscious wants, ask other people to observe you and give you feedback. What was the impression you made? Now I'm not suggesting you get self-obsessed here, but if you are unsure about the signals you projected, only someone else who was present can give you feedback. Admit your uncertainty to them. They may be very helpful in giving you insights into your own unconscious. And when you are creating something, any sort of project that takes more than a day or two, a diary or journal, where you jot down both your own responses and those of other people, can be a really helpful way of revealing how your unconscious might be helping or hindering your progress.

Finally, you stop yourself from using your unconscious as a creative storehouse when you fail to acknowledge its existence, fail to give it attention and experience strong clashes between your unconscious and conscious goals. Just realising the power of the unconscious and acknowledging its influence – noticing its effects on others and ourselves, and seeing how profoundly memories, stories and metaphors help us make sense of the world – will put you into a much stronger creative mood. Rather than some dark, unfathomable place where demons and shadows lurk, your unconscious can be a powerful resource and ally in making brilliant ideas happen. You may never really know your unconscious – but this chapter should have given you some ideas about how to nurture it.

With your unconscious primed, you can now go on to the next vital stage of making brilliant ideas happen: creating a vision.

4

Creating a Vision

Believing — Immersing — Idea generating — Creating a Vision — Reality checking — Piloting — Realising

This chapter is about its title and believing, again.

What happens to a dream deferred?

> *Does it dry up*
> *Like a raisin in the sun?*
> *Or fester like a sore –*
> *And then run?*
> *Does it stink like rotten meat?*
> *Or crust and sugar over –*
> *Like a syrupy sweet?*
> *Maybe it just sags*
> *Like a heavy load*
> *Or does it explode?*
>
> – Langston Hughes

I love this wonderfully threatening poem. If your dream idea is going to 'dry up', 'fester', 'stink and crust', then surely it is better to take the easier path, and realise it, isn't it? This chapter is all about realising your dream idea, and throughout it you may experience a strange sense of 'something is missing here'. Realising your idea is all about 'what is possible'. What is missing from this chapter is a sense of 'what is not possible'. We are talking about two different brain activities here: the first one being about constructing, imagining and taking leaps of faith, the second about analysing, thinking critically and seeking criticism. To make your brilliant ideas happen, you need to do both. But possibly the most important skill in developing creative intelligence is the ability to separate these two activities. So please, for this chapter, silence your critical gremlins – they will be let out in Chapter Five – and fasten your seat belt. Let's get on with a trip of total possibility.

Now Picasso wanted to create a painting. He wanted it to be green. So he went outside, walked around, and looked and looked at everything green. He blitzed himself with green, immersed himself in it totally, till he was almost nauseous with greenness. Then he went and created his painting. The greenness he described as 'bursting out of him'.

This story is by way of a reminder of an earlier theme in this book, that we want to create what we love, which we feel motivated by and passionate about. You won't have a vision unless you are so steeped in something that it blitzes you with content. This creative vision will arise as a result of believing in yourself, being immersed in your subject and your having played around a lot with ideas. It will appear when those ideas come together to make a coherent whole.

A vision keeps you going through the inevitable ups and downs of the creative process; it engages your emotions and imagination. But, perhaps more importantly, when an idea is presented in vision form to other people, it gets their emotions and imaginations engaged, too. A vision is the secret to turning other people on – it reminds us just how much we have in common with one another, and how we all need hope.

'Vision' is one of those big, loaded, abstract words that is open to lots of different interpretations. In an organisation, a chief executive can have a vision, which leaves employees thinking: 'yes, that may be a good vision for planet Zog, where the Chief Executive seems to live, but we are all actually on Earth, having to implement the thing'. Corporate visions work best when they are created by the people who have to implement them, rather than by a boss who has overdosed on new management theory.

The best visions are based on what people believe, value and know to be important in life. A vision is an end result involving the imagination. Its definition is about imagery and that which will be *seen*. A target is not the same as a vision, because it almost always involves numbers and quantifying objects. People are not motivated by targets, unless they represent something symbolic that is important to them: the money to buy a new house, a sense of one-upmanship or a measure of collective achievement, for instance. People are motivated by visions, because they create stories for the future, which give us hope: a very necessary emotion. But visions are also based on what has happened in the past; we recognise metaphors and memories, both conscious and unconscious, in them. Your vision will be essentially qualitative.

Visions like Margaret Thatcher's 'property owning democracy' or Tony Blair's 'stakeholder society' present us with ideas that we are already familiar with: a fair world where everyone owns their own home, or a fair world where everyone's voice is heard and people feel a sense of ownership about their contribution to society. Both visions are about owning, but in the first it is about houses, from someone who was quoted as saying she did not believe in such a thing as society, the second is about owning vested interests in a society that he believes, categorically, does exist.

eureka!

A vision is what you want to bring into being. It is not something you feel dutiful about having, or that society, your family or friends tell you that you should want. It cannot be foisted on you. It is something that builds inside your mind as you piece information, experience, imagination and passion together. Robert Fritz, the writer and composer, defines a vision as an 'organising principle'. It is an outcome, from which we organise backwards. I like this definition very much, because, rather than some lofty abstract concept, it suggests that a vision is a trigger for action. I can't emphasise enough how important it is to have a vision before you start to create anything. If you get stuck, it may be a sign that you are not sufficiently immersed in your subject and you haven't gathered enough good-quality information about it. Or it may be a sign that, unconsciously, you are not really sure you want to do it. You may not completely believe that it is an area in which you'd be wise to spend time and energy. Your imagination and emotions may be refusing to engage in the idea, fully – in which case, it is time to look elsewhere.

Seeing Yourself as an Originator

People who lack confidence to express ideas usually do not see themselves as originators – that is, people who bring events into being rather than just react to events around them.

There are many books written on creativity, which assume that creative intelligence is the ability to solve problems. But, while creative thinking is one way of solving problems, creative intelligence is much more than this. Creative intelligence involves bringing into being something new, rather than merely moving away from some difficulty. This difference of emphasis is crucial, I think. When we bring something new into being, we move both psychologically and physically, as well as time-wise, towards it. In contrast when we solve a problem, we are orientated very differently – to moving away psychologically and physically from the problem and to doing so as quickly as possible.

When we are using our creativity, our point of origin is the thing we wish to make or create; when we problem-solve, our point of origin is the thing we wish to avoid. We feel more powerful in the first instance; it is *our minds* which shape and design. In the second instance, it is the *problem* that can seem most powerful – and overwhelming and dominant in its complexity. It is the difference between J.K. Rowling thinking 'there are not many gripping and magical stories written that children and adults would both like to read' and her thinking 'I have this amazing tale and characters bursting out of my head, which I would love to share with others'. I am only guessing, but the second sentiment sounds a lot more likely to me than the first.

To use your creative intelligence, then, you have to believe that you can bring things into being, that you can make things happen. We know from something called attribution theory that successful people tend to attribute success more to their own efforts, than to the effects of chance and opportunity. And there tend to be differences between the sexes in how they attribute their success: more men than women attributing it to their own abilities, while women focus more on the roles of luck and opportunity. Psychology also described something called 'locus of control': which is about the extent to which we believe as individuals we can be instrumental in initiating and changing things. Predictably enough, those people with a strong locus of control tend to be a lot more successful than those without. You'll probably have heard of the phrase 'learned helplessness' meaning a dependency that someone tends to use and rely on, which stops them doing anything for themselves. The highly creative have never learnt helplessness, unless perhaps it is in domestic or practical chores, which distract them from their purpose . . . They see themselves as proactive, able to initiate, with a strong locus of control. This is not the same at all as an outward show of confidence. It is about inner belief.

So, in order to use your creative intelligence, you have to believe that you can originate, that you can work with a blank page. However, seeing yourself as a champion problem-solver, with the marks on the page already made, may work against this. You may become accustomed to your point of origin being a problem, which you habitually respond to. Where there does not appear to be a problem, or the problem is difficult to define, you will feel as if you have no point of origin. In creative intelligence workshops, I constantly see this reaction when participants are asked to tell stories. Managerial types, who regard themselves primarily as 'problem-solvers', feel confused and uncertain when asked to originate stories. They have forgotten what it feels like to create points of origin themselves.

If you want to draw your vision, or write a book, or create a business, then this may mean literally getting comfortable with blank pages or blank Microsoft word documents on your computer screen. But, for others, blank pages may be more metaphorical: the empty diary, the dissolving of routine, the lack of phone calls and contact from people who used to be clients or customers. You need to get comfortable with these sensations of blankness and emptiness and not feel that you have to run around, headless-chicken-like, in order to fill these voids. One of the most useful metaphors for these blank pages or voids can be to think of them as clearing. Were you to build a hut in a clearing, then charging in and chucking together everything that is available would be unwise. The best way to build this hut is to sit, contemplate the space it will occupy, think about what would work best there, and then structure how you will use your available resources.

Traditional IQ testing prizes analysis and critical thinking –

that is, the ability to think about the downside of possibilities and what could go wrong. Too much of this kills creative intelligence before it gets off the ground. You never try anything or make any marks on the blank page, in case they are not 'right'. You might look silly. You are only comfortable correcting marks others have already made. Your love of negative analysis makes you a fantastic critic, who never suggests constructive alternatives – which is, of course, what really clever, creative people do.

In the business world, because of the over-emphasis on IQ, people frequently use negative analysis in inappropriate contexts, in order to look clever and maintain their image of having 'intelligence'. Vittorio Radice, is a real contender for 'most creatively intelligent business leader in the UK'; he revolutionised first Habitat, and then the more prestigious Selfridges. He turned Selfridges from a rather old-fashioned department store into an extraordinarily exciting shopping theatre. At the time of writing, Vittorio has taken over the homeware division of Marks and Spencer, and is planning to open new large homeware stores. Of his plans, a city analyst commented in *The Times*: 'Where is the competitive edge in these plans? Where is the detail?'. Clearly, this analyst, as befits his job title, has no understanding that creative intelligence involves origination first, rather than problem-solving, which comes later – that is, worrying about the competition. Creative business people like Vittorio put out new ideas, first and foremost, and it is through the inventiveness of this 'putting out of ideas' that they see off any competition, rather than through a reactive orientation to others in the marketplace. The reaction can follow later.

To make brilliant ideas happen, you have to see yourself as someone who brings things into being on blank pages. Sometimes this may involve ignoring problems in your surroundings, and just concentrating on finding the space to originate. It may involve holding back until you are absolutely ready to assemble your ideas into a vision, or waiting until you

eureka!

feel it is wanting to burst out of you, so that you have no alternative but to express it.

STAGE 7

The eureka programme: originating your vision

1. Every time you have an idea, jot it down in a notebook. Then periodically stop, and put these ideas together into picture form, on a large blank sheet of paper. Do you have a vision here? Do certain ideas need greater prominence, while others need to be edited? Keep doing this over a period of time, until your vision appears coherent in other words, – like a satisfactory whole.

2. Your vision needs to fit totally into the context of how you see yourself living in the future, so take time for some reflection here. What are the best decisions you have made in your life? Write them down, then ask yourself what beliefs and values were behind those decisions? What matters to you most in life? Remind yourself of what you would like to do, if you knew you were leaving this planet in six months. You will find it useful to reflect on these matters over a few days, or even a few weeks. Include sketches of your personal and professional life. Is there a vision in here that you can hone in on? Write down a description of how you would like to be living and working in three years time, and write it in the present tense. Visions are much more likely to be realised when they are described on paper than when they are not. You put them out into the ether, that way, and, I suspect, etch them more vividly onto your unconscious.

---

3. Think slowly and deeply about what you would like to do in your life, and spend as long as you need to at a blank sheet of paper, or a blank computer screen. Get used to looking at this blankness and do not put anything down there until you are absolutely certain of key points that you want to illustrate or write down. Just put down those bare bones, and nothing more.

4. By now you should know what you believe in and value in life, what you know about and, most crucially, what you love to do. Sketch all of these on a piece of a paper. Then you can find a vision through asking the question: 'What could be possible here?' There are many different ways in which you can represent a vision. Drawing it is one way, obviously, or modelling something in plasticine. On workshops, we often suggest to people that they make a collage out of magazine illustrations and advertisements for something they want to create in their lives. Then we ask other participants to comment on what they see. Quite often, participants are inspired sufficiently by their collages to take them back to their offices or homes, and stick them on the wall. Robert Fritz encourages people to create visions out of objects they may have in their bags, or which are scattered around a room. He says there is a big difference between the results that different kinds of people get. Those who organize their visions in their minds, and are clear about what they want to create before they start, produce very different results from those people who just plunge in and make something without thinking. As we might suspect, the former present the more coherent visions.

5. As part of building a more creative orientation, you can become a more confident originator through changing your approach to problem-solving. Every time you are presented with a problem that is not immediately urgent, take a beat or two to check your usual response of 'what can be done to solve this problem?' and ask yourself 'what could I create to push this problem to one side?' or 'what could I bring into being here?' I am not suggesting that this will always give you solutions, but it will get you out of your habitual ways of responding.

6. Sam came on a workshop and said:

'I always have problems creating a vision, not with the actual activity, but with what I put into it. There are always a lot of money signs. And I don't like to think of myself as a greedy person, but money is quite important to me. It makes me feel uneasy that I can't really be honest, and that I don't like what's down there . . .'

Worrying about social approval won't help you create an honest vision. So when you are getting your vision down on paper, suspend all critical judgement. This is an indulgent flight of fancy for you, where no-one, least of all yourself, is censoring the dream. But when you look at what's down there, and experience feelings like those Sam describes, ask yourself 'what does money mean to me?' and 'have I paid sufficient attention to relationships?' Money may symbolise a good quality of life, with a lovely home, or greater freedom to choose how you spend your time, or one-upmanship with your neighbours. Also, money and relationships often fit together. Someone who was passionate about their business once told me that expanding a business was really about finding just how many people in the world you had things in common with.

7. Put yourself into a visionary orientation. Talk to others about their visions and how close they are to fulfilling them, read stories of people who have had successful visions in your chosen subject area, pay particular attention to new stories about people who have succeeded with their visions. Now I'm not trying to turn you into Joan of Arc here, but your antennae may benefit from vision-sensitising.

Art, Science and Limitations

When I was in school, decades ago, we had to opt to do either arts or sciences at A-level. This was a shame for people like me, who loved English, History and Maths, but were prevented from doing the latter. Instead, I took French, which I loathed and feared. And I still have a recurring nightmare about going to sit my French A-level exam, having in my dream somehow missed the entire syllabus . . . Nowadays, we are more enlightened about the school curriculum, but some of us may have unwittingly fallen into art or science without thinking about the differences – and, more importantly, the similarities – between the two.

In defining a vision, it is useful to be clear about the extent to which it is an artistic or a scientific one, or rather, like this book, straddling the two as an interesting hybrid. And it is worth asking ourselves whether we are working under unnecessary limitations in seeing ourselves as artists or scientists. Could you become an interesting hybrid yourself? Is it time to release your inner Renaissance woman or man?

Does creativity work differently in different areas – like art and science? At the time of writing, the boundaries between art and science are becoming a growing area of interest and investigation. In the UK, we have NESTA, the National Endowment for Science, Technology and the Arts, backing projects like Antartic Waves, an interactive CD teaching resource that teaches science through music composition. The Sciart Project, funded by the Wellcome Trust, is spending a million pounds on supporting and encouraging innovative arts projects connected with bio-medical issues.

Scientists and artists start with an idea. The scientist might call it a hypothesis, or an idea of a link between at least one thing and another. Both then experiment to test their idea or hypothesis. Scientific and artistic thinking uses a basic unit – a ratio – that is, the proportion of one thing to another. Most of us can remember the thrill of making scientific potions in chemistry, in the science lab, mixing specific amounts of different chemicals to produce a noxious fizzing potion. In painting, writing and music, composition ratio is the funda- mental unit employed. It may relate to the relative size of different parts of a painting, the intensity of the colour in one area to another, how much description is given to a heroine's home and the extent to which her inner dialogue is described compared to other characters, how much of a composition is in a major or minor key and whether a section is to be played in andante or allegro style. Ratio exists because of structure.

Both science and art require structure. The bare bones of either type of endeavour, and the clarity of these basic elements, will be a key part of what is conveyed to others. Perhaps science strives more for clarity and simplicity than art. Scientists often speak of theories having elegance or beauty because of their clarity and simplicity. Art, on the other hand, often concerns itself with ambiguity and complexity, but this must arise from a deep structure.

Science and art have more in common than is often thought. To be innovative in science, you must produce a theory, some- thing conceptual and abstract, although of course this may result in something concrete like a Dyson hoover or a new pharmaceutical compound. To create in art, you will need to translate your ideas into something tangible like a piece of music, a design, a novel or a painting. Both science and art are sold, as in business.

You may find it helpful to think about the organisation in which you are involved. Is it in the private or public sector? Is there too much emphasis on science or art in what you are trying to do?

People are motivated by different inclinations in their quest to become artists or scientists. Artists – and I mean this in the broadest sense – often believe they are transmitting a particularly individual and unique vision to the world. They may be tempted to overlook the fact that, for their vision to have any relevance for anyone else, it has to carry universal elements and qualities. Scientists may believe that they are taking some universal truth to the world, although, since chaos theory, and light waves being seen as both particles and waves, scientists have increasingly acknowledged that they present their truths via paradigms – that is, particular ways of seeing the world. It is widely acknowledged that it is impossible to separate commentary about what is being observed from the person doing the observing.

But great ideas in art, science and business all have a characteristic coherence about them: that is, their structural elements are obvious and they hang together well. In business, producing brilliant ideas will involve art and science. Anita Roddick needed science to produce her Body Shop potions and the arts of shop design, customer relations and publicity to sell them. James Dyson's vacuum cleaner relied on science and engineering to get it working, but again, the arts of design and marketing sold if for him. In art, science and business, you will need to bring your ideas to communal judgement. There may be greater peer group pressure in the scientific community, where peer review and the modification and acceptance of ideas is critical. The critical market for artistic creations may be less obvious but it is suggested, for instance, that 10,000 people in London and New York create the art market through what they buy, write about and trade in. In business, you may be bringing your idea to the judgement of an established market, or blazing a trail and identifying a new market for your idea, telling people that they want it whether they realise it or not.

Many of our greatest creators did not view themselves with the limiting tag of 'scientist' or 'artist'. Aristotle was a scientist and a drama critic, Einstein a physicist and a wordsmith. Leonardo da Vinci painted the Mona Lisa and designed a flying machine, helicopter and parachute, amongst other inventions. The abstract painter Jackson Pollock performed sets of complex algebraic equations, firing up his brain with the exercise of structure before painting. Anita Roddick regards herself as both campaigner and businesswoman, James Dyson as designer, engineer, businessman and salesperson. But my favourite modern-day creator has to be Bruce Dickinson. Not satisfied with being front man for the globally successful heavy metal band Iron Maiden, he has published children's stories, works as a radio presenter and has qualified as a fully fledged airline pilot. If you fly with Easyjet, you may be lucky enough to have him in your cockpit.

These creators all spent time studying different areas and investigated crossing over the boundaries between subjects. Many great ideas occur at boundaries: in the UK, the sandwich shop Prêt a Manger is on the boundary of your local delicatessen and McDonalds, selling top-quality fresh food at reasonable prices in many outlets. Great ideas do not just have coherence within them, in that their structures are very definite. They are also well placed in their environments and where they fit in the world is clear.

STAGE 8

The eureka programme: science, art and boundaries

1. Are you, by inclination, more of an artist or scientist? Could your vision benefit from more art or science? Scientists are generally rigorously trained to infer from nothing other than what they observe, in order to work out how things work. Often, they can benefit from also paying attention to feelings, ideas that cannot be verbalised and what seems beautiful or ugly in their work. Great scientists are always passionate about research and discovery, and their inventions always involve metaphor and imagery, to some degree. Dialogue with artists about their subject matter can be illuminating about the extent to which we interact with the world via our senses, as well as our traditional IQ. Read Candace Pert's *The Molecules of Emotion* for a wonderful account of passion, fear, loathing and fantasies across the Bunsen burners.

   Artists are often rigorously trained to use their senses and subjectivity to inspire what they wish to communicate. They can also benefit from applying the scientist's experimental approach to how what they are creating fits in objective reality. Who would want what they have created, where would it fit and what facts are already known about the market? Artists can pretend facts don't exist and create art that has no truth, truth being what we think about facts. But they are unlikely to become successful. A scientific approach to what's out there can help the artist get real and base their visions on truth – the best basis for interpretation. Scientists can benefit from becoming more outwardly expressive, and artists can benefit from developing forensic skills.

So, if you are to get all artistic about your vision, imagine how it would be in sensory terms. How would you, and it, look, feel, sound? What emotions would it produce in you and others? To get forensic and scientific about it, go to where you would enact your vision, if at all possible, and imagine yourself in that context, realising the vision. How does it fit there?

2. Draw your vision of your idea, and put boundaries around it with distinct lines. What lies in your border territories? What surrounds your vision in its world? What will you name your vision? It needs to be called something succinct, which neatly sums up for you what it is about. How will your vision look to others in the border territories? Who can help you implement it? Are there people lurking on the borders of your vision who can give you advice and tell you what they think about it?

3. Cultivate whatever it is you must do in order to have visions. If you get them in daydreams, which you enjoy, then daydream more. If you love to make them concrete through doodling or written descriptions, then doodle and describe more. Enjoy the fact that you can surf across those unconscious and conscious neurons, without any niggling critic interfering.

Setting Goals

So what's the difference between your vision and your goals? Well, your vision describes a whole outcome and lurks in the imagination, emotions and senses, making it difficult to measure. You know when you've arrived there by feeling 'yes, this is exactly where I wanted to be'. Your goals will be key elements of your vision, and they will be tangible and measurable. Your goals will fit in with the above process and they will have time deadlines, and possibly mini-goals, en route.

Jim manages several stores, which are trading badly. He researches the problem and finds out that his staff are demoralised and uninterested in what they are doing. He creates a vision in his mind and on paper of a much more motivated workforce, improved store interiors, far better customer relations and, of course, profits soaring. His goals, which will be measurable, are improved morale, better feedback from customers and a cash target. His mini-goals become:

First six months: Embark on motivating and training staff and starting store improvements.

By end of first year: Completion of store improvements and start customer relations programme.

By end of second year: Hit cash targets, complete improvements and measure improved morale of both staff and customers.

Factors in the ever-changing trading environment, of course, will need to be monitored. So, keep checking whether these mini-goals remain realistic.

STAGE 9

The eureka programme: process and goals

1. When you get stuck trying to make your ideas happen, check the actions described in the CQ-building process: believing, immersing, idea-generating, creating a vision, reality checking, selling and realising. Have you got stuck somewhere? Can you move to a different activity in order to get unstuck?

2. Draw your vision as vividly as you can and identify three key elements in it. Now translate these into specific goals; write them down and plan, time-wise, when you will achieve them. If useful, plan mini-goals, stages on the way, in your diary. Remember, these are not written in stone and reality-checking may mean that you have to alter them. But they will provide you with a good, strong skeleton. You will find it helpful to get some feedback about your vision before you start trying to practically realise your goals.

The Sustaining Power of Your Vision

I suspect this may be one of the most important messages in this book.

The vision you have created will help you get organised. It is something that will pull you and your energies and focus in a certain direction. It will help you notice things in the world and your immediate surroundings that you have not seen before. Deep inside your imagination, it will help you prioritise what you should do and who you should be spending time with. It will constantly remind you of 'what is possible'.

In describing how to build CQ, I am asking you to play three distinctive roles. I am asking you to be a creator or builder, which is what this chapter has been about, a researcher and a critic or evaluator, which the next chapter will be about. Being successfully creative involves balancing these three roles and developing your capacities for generating possibilities and seeking and using criticism. People who make their ideas happen – often in the face of great criticism and discouragement from others – keep remembering their role as a creator or builder. They use their vision to sustain themselves and to pick themselves up after knocks. It is their vision that keeps them going, when the going gets really tough. So be sure your vision is one that is really worthwhile, one that you will want to live with for a very long time, and one that you are prepared to sweat over. Then cherish it. Keep a representation of it, sketch or description, readily available in a notebook. Then remind yourself of it whenever you need a boost.

It is vision which gives us courage, and boldness, and helps us take risks. Rupert Murdoch, the media mogul, was sustained through near bankruptcy and giant industrial relations problems at Wapping by his vision of a global media village. The Saatchi brothers, advertising agency kings, had no employees when they started off. But a potential client wanted to visit their office, so they hired people off the street to sit in the office and pretend to be working there. When Anita Roddick first opened her Body Shop, she sprayed strawberry essence on the route to the shop in order to pull customers in. A clear vision seems to give people unexpected resourcefulness.

This vision will be a sustaining top priority. But the critical function matters too. So let's now move on to look at building CQ though dealing with those voices – our own and other people's – that say 'that's just not possible!'.

5

Critical Demons – and Others

Believing — *Immersing* — *Idea generating* — *Creating a Vision* — *Reality-checking* — *Piloting* — *Realising*

This chapter is about reality-checking.

Caroline works for an IT company and has come up with an idea to improve service delivery. She is thrilled with this idea, schemes it out in great detail on paper and takes it to her boss. 'Won't work, Caroline,' he says, 'too time-consuming.' Caroline gets very upset. 'Don't be silly, Caroline,' says her boss. 'It's not you I'm criticising – it's your idea.'

'Yes,' she says, 'I understand that intellectually, but emotionally, it hurts. I was deeply in love with that idea and it does feel like a part of me . . . I need your help and support with this.' The boss looks embarrassed . . .

There is no way of avoiding it. We now have to deal with the 'ouch' subject: criticism. Tempted though you may be to skip over this chapter, stick with it please. What you read could change your life. We are going to look at self-criticism: how you analyse and reject aspects of your own ideas. We will look at other self-generated gremlins that may blight your success, too. And we are going to look at how we get and respond to criticism from other people, a vital part of developing creative intelligence and making your brilliant ideas happen.

When I write a book, I always run workshops to implement the ideas I'm exploring on a practical level. Such workshops are vital to the content of a book of this nature; they tell me what people's concerns and difficulties are in every day reality. They remind me that all the theorising in the world is fine, but useless, if people can't put the ideas into practice. Now I'm not saying all of this to make me sound especially virtuous; it's just that in the pilot workshops for this book, there were two recurring themes that people talked about. The first was that if we, as individuals, are too self-critical early on in exploring an idea, then that idea never gets off the ground. The possibilities of what could go wrong prevent our schemes from ever taking flight.

The second theme that people mentioned a great deal was a fear of criticism. Fantasies about others pouring scorn on the idea, or laughing hysterically at it were very common. Yet of course, criticism – or the nice version of the word, feed-back – is the only way we can learn how our ideas are being received. It is through criticism that we understand how our visions can fit reality. This may be perverse, but I want to help you get addicted to this form of reality-checking, so that you even learn to enjoy it.

One of the key criteria for successful enterprises – be they small businesses, voluntary organisations, government agencies, global conglomerates or sole traders – is the extent to which they engage with criticism. It is the only way in which we can tell how what we are trying to do is being received in the outside environment. Research shows that successful companies are those that confront 'brutal realities'.

Being Your Own Best Critic

Before you ask others to act as critics of your idea, it is wise to play the role of critic yourself. I am sure that one of the key skills of people who are highly creative and productive is the ability to separate the activities of idea-generating, where they are taking leaps of possibility and building visions, from the activity of criticising themselves. During idea-generating, the critic must be silent and asleep. During criticism, the idea-generator must be calm and uninvolved.

Your inner critic needs to act as a critical best friend might. Most of us have distinctive preoccupations, which are top priorities for us in our endeavours. They are qualities that we 'care most about being found out not to be'. We may be very keen to be clear or competent, or distinctively individual, or very appealing to others, for instance. We need to be especially aware when we think critically about our own work, that we do not become obsessive about these preoccupations. For instance, if you are obsessed with distinctive individuality, and criticising a product you have developed, you risk making it so unusual and individual that others will have problems relating it to their needs. Remember that only a small percentage of the population is likely to share your particular fixation.

As a critical best friend, your inner critical eye should take a look at your idea and ask 'what is working here?' and 'what is not working?' Self-criticism should always start with some positives; otherwise, you have nothing constructive to build on. But a lot of us have not been conditioned to take criticism or give it in this way. We immediately rush to identify short-comings. This critical eye should also be good at spotting others who are doing what you want to do, or something similar, and thereby identifying useful role models.

STAGE 10

The eureka programme: training your best critic

1. You can use imaginative techniques to separate your idea-generating thinking from your critical thinking. If it helps, give each function a character and a personality: make the idea-generator a cheerful, open-minded, energetic individual (Bill Clinton, perhaps, if he appeals . . .) and the critical thinker a focussed, cool and analytical individual (Hillary, perhaps?). Then you can choose whether to activate your inner Bill or Hillary! Visualise them taking over your brain.

2. Limit the amount of time you spend criticising via the criteria of your obsession, if you have one. Think about other people you know well and the way they criticise things, and imagine how they would comment on your idea. Perhaps you have a partner like mine who is very keen to criticise on the basis of the question: how well does this work?' Identify for yourself the questions that others whom you know well would ask.

3. When you are critically reviewing something you have done, train yourself to make notes in two columns. The first must cover what worked, and the second can describe scope for improvement. Ask yourself: 'What could I have done differently here?'

4. When you look at people you admire, or who are role models for you, avoid becoming preoccupied with what they have achieved. Instead, ask yourself: 'What have they done to achieve this? What process was involved?' The next Anita Roddick or James Dyson will not produce environmentally friendly cosmetics or amazing designer vacuum cleaners; they will produce something in a different context. But the means, or

> process, or what they do to get there may well be very similar to that of their own role models.

Getting Criticism From Others

While if you feel passionate and committed to your idea, you are far more likely to make it happen, these emotions can make criticism hard to take. Caring a great deal about an idea can make you hyper-sensitive about it, so that both praise and negative comments become overly significant. But the only way we have of reality-checking our ideas is by going out and asking people what they think of them. You can call it feedback, or evaluation, which may soften the blow, but what we are really still talking about here is getting criticism. And it is the only way of finding out whether your idea will really work or not.

I suspect that sensitivity to criticism is the one single barrier that stops many people from bringing their ideas to fruition. We are too reluctant to risk what seems like personal rejection. But criticism does not only serve to give us feedback on our ideas, and input on how we can modify them: it also creates champions, advertisers and markets for our ideas. Once people get involved with what we are doing and give advice on it, they are far more likely to tell others about it. Asking people for criticism gets them telling and selling.

Jane is head of training in a food company, and says:

A few years ago, I became very keen on the idea that we ran an after-hours 'extra learning' club for employees who wanted to further develop themselves. I suspected that quite a few of the directors would regard this as 'yet another pointless HR initiative' so I decided I would involve them early on in the process. I set out very clearly how the club would work practically, and then asked them what they thought the advantages and disadvan-

tages might be. Just a week or two after I'd done this, people started to approach me from all parts of the business, wanting to join the club. My asking for criticism had meant I had effectively cut out any need for selling the idea to the employees – because their bosses had thought through the repercussions of it. This bunch of sceptical directors even became competitive about how many employees they could encourage to join the club!

When someone offers criticism – wanted or unwanted – they are just giving you their response to your idea. That's all it is really, some critical thinking from *them* about something *you* have put out into the world. Their criticism will reflect their own priorities regarding what's important, as will your re-action. So if you are most concerned about being seen as an expert and they criticise you on the basis of naivete and ignorance, your reaction will be a strong one. I am reiterating the point here – that you need to know what obsesses you most – because it makes you vulnerable. If you know this, when you get criticism from someone who you believe to be obsessive about something, then you can keep that opinion of yours to yourself or put it in its rightful place.

Just offering negative criticism is quite easy, of course. It is just about saying 'well, this, this and this is wrong'. The usefulness of criticism to you, oh creators, though, is in what it tells you could be done differently. So, as a recipient of criticism, your most useful question will be 'and how do you think I could do this differently?'

STAGE 11

The eureka programme: taking criticism impersonally

1. Remember, negative criticism is better than no reaction at all. At least someone has got involved with your idea.

And the person's comments may be useful, a) to improve your idea or b) in realising that this person has an obsession or agenda you want little to do with. Being given triggers to improve your idea gives you yet another opportunity to go back to the creative drawing board, to be resourceful and inventive again . . .

2. I have already made this point, but *you* are not your idea. The two things exist separately. Current estimates regarding the complexity of the personality give it 5,000 aspects – so, by that reckoning, a great deal of you will not be reflected in your idea.

3. If you do feel upset, ring-fence time to be upset, vow vengeance on the individual and fantasise about it, but don't act on this. Give yourself a half-hour 'fret-time' once a day, and if you take this while at the gym, you may find it improves performance. Imagine sending the offender a witty note or e-mail or something surprising in the post. And you don't have to have read *The Godfather*, where the mafia send someone a horse's head, to come up with ideas here. Talk to others about your reaction and make it humorous if you can.

4. Wear an imaginary flak jacket when people give you criticism. It will be duvet-lined, in your favourite colour, and smell of wonderful things like chocolate, vanilla and lime. It will form an invisible protective bubble around you, so that whatever barbs they throw at you, you will still feel good.

5. Seek criticism from a sufficient cross-section of people. A bad reaction can motivate you to swiftly get some more opinions, from people who are not so mealy-mouthed.

6. You have a choice. Is your vision of your idea more important than your feeling a bit hurt, or vice versa? Just do it . . . and tough it out . . . These comments come from a person who has moved on from a press review she got over the summer of a TV show she presents which opened with the line 'Why is Philippa Davies so annoying?',and went downhill from there!!!! Remember, you're learning. You only do that through knowing the negative shortfall between where you are now, and where you want to be.

7. Densensitisation works. Get used to asking people for criticism and just listening to what they say without any strong reaction, apart from interest. Keep telling yourself 'I'm interested in this'. Then take away their comments and reflect on them,. coolly and quietly. Notice your reactions, and what your uncon-scious may be telling your about their opinions.

Setting up criticism

Terry is a friend of mine who has written about 20 books. He is a very open, spontaneous character and, when he was finding it hard to get a publishing deal for his latest novel, asked a friend for advice. The friend suggested he show the manuscript to some mutual acquaintances who bought and sold ideas commercially in various forms. Terry followed this advice but, being a rather over-the-top sort of character, sent his manu-script to six people, rather than the two the friend suggested. Unfortunately, what he omitted to do was to ask people if they would like to take up the role of critic.

You can probably guess what happened. Two friends were horrified, felt ill-equipped to judge a manuscript and did not want to compromise their friendship with Terry by saying what they really felt. A couple struggled to read the manuscript, even though it was an unfamiliar genre to them and nothing they would ever want to buy or read. And a couple conferred, agreed they hated the book, and then agreed on similar constructive feedback, which probably gave Terry the impression he was much more likely to get a publishing deal than was really the case . . .

Which all goes to show that getting criticism needs to be a tactical business. Here are some suggested tactics:

You can time it right. Whatever you show to people for criticism, it needs to be in a form that will enable them to see quite easily how the finished idea will look, sound, feel and operate. Showing them something half-baked, which requires a lot of imagination to conceive of the end result, risks them becoming overly and destructively critical. So time your request for when you feel that whatever you are working on is clearly an embryonic version of your final vision. And be sensitive to demands on their time; they may like you to leave your idea with them, so they can have a good think about it. They can then chat through with you their responses at a time of their choosing.

You can ask the right people. It can be very difficult to find people who will bother to find the time to look at what you are doing, and who do not feel embarrassed by your request. They don't have to be people you like. In fact, asking people with whom you have a very friendly relationship may make the task harder, as they will be reluctant to say anything that may hurt you. The best people to ask are those whose opinion you respect, who are knowledgeable and influential in your field and whose opinions and ways of seeing things are unpredictable and refreshing. Unlike Terry, it is best to ask people who are likely to be interested in your idea, or who are likely to use a specific service or product, or who sell ideas themselves.

In my experience, it helps if you acknowledge why you are

asking specific individuals for their opinions, and encourage them to be as frank as possible. It is also worth showing your appreciation for their time. Generally speaking, the great majority of people are conservative and resistant to change, so it is worth remembering.

You can use the right question. You may be lucky enough to know people who will give you a full and useful account of their opinions when asked the big, general question: 'what do you think of it?' Others may need more specific directions like: 'do you think the plot works?' or 'do you think the bank manager will think this plan is viable?' Where you have reservations or sense weaknesses, it may be worth mentioning them too, so you can get your instincts confirmed and contradicted.

The giving of criticism itself can be made into a creative activity, with questions like 'if you were doing this, how would you have done it differently?' – which, as an exercise, is useful imagining – or 'is there anything there should be more or less of, which you think would improve this?'

You can appreciate what the criticism means. Criticism tells you a lot about the giver. It tells you what is important to them, what they value, the perspective from which they view life and how they see things. An eminent academic who came on one of my workshops was typical of many experts: he gave all his criticism based on how others could make their work more like *his*. He was using his own approach as a definitive standard, from which others were deviating . . . We will all do this to a certain extent, our critical criteria inevitably reflecting our own priorities. But useful criticism will have a breadth to it, and often include comments from a couple of different perspectives. People who can do this are rare and valuable, so if you come across such a critic, nurture them.

You can clarify the criticism. When people feel anxious about something, they often hear less well. You may find it difficult to understand what people are getting at when they comment on your ideas, because you care so much about them. Ask for clarification if necessary, and remember that criticism is most useful when it is phrased in verbs – as being what you could do differently.

You can regard all responses as useful. When you have an idea, you need to put it about a bit, to talk to as many people as possible about it and to get their input. Throw-away comments, lack of interest, jokey responses or incredulity that you should be contemplating such a scheme are all informative responses. You need to be hyper-sensitive to everything that people say or don't say, while reminding yourself that it is your idea that people are commenting on, rather than your entire being.

You can rumble agendas. There is a useful technique for handling people who you think might be giving negative criticism as part of a nastier agenda: engage with them further. Ask them to be more specific, if they could talk you through how your idea could be improved, if they would mind expanding on the idea's shortcomings. Where there is a nastier agenda, you will almost always find that this request makes them go away . . .

And remember, you always have the right to think: 'I've always secretly believed that person who criticised my idea was a dork – now I've got my confirmation.'

Irrepressibility

The BBC 2 television series 'Mind of a Millionaire' showed very successful entrepreneurs undergoing various psychological tests in order to work out whether there was a distinctive 'success' mindset. The founders of the do-it-yourself chain B & Q were featured. They had sold the business in its relative infancy for about £5 million, and gone off to do other things. One was once more a multi-millionaire and the other had very little. The TV psychologists and we, the viewers, were invited to guess who was who.

One founder seemed sharp, analytical and business-like. He had gone to Guernsey to grow tomatoes and the business had failed, due to bad weather and other factors. The other founder, who was more reflective, avuncular and slightly bumbly had established a china business. 'It was a disaster,' he said 'I knew nothing about manufacturing china.'

Like the TV psychologists, I was tempted to believe, because of his self-presentation, that the sharper, more analytical man had once more created a fortune. But we were wrong. It was the avuncular founder, who had subsequently moved on from disastrous china, to establish a hugely successful video business, just as video hire was starting to become very popular. His distinguishing characteristic, it was pointed out, was the ability to take the blame.

One of the distinguishing characteristics of successful people is how they explain what has happened to them in life. Psychology calls it attribution theory. Successful people tend to attribute failure to their own shortcomings, rather than blaming influences from other people, the environment or fate. Logically, then, this means they can do something about the failure through behaving differently in the future. The failure is viewed as useful criticism about how to get the idea right next time. Taking responsibility for what has gone wrong makes these people successful. In characteristic fashion, Body Shop founder Anita Roddick did not hold back when asked about the failure of her restaurant, Paddingtons, which she opened prior to the Body Shop: 'We had done everything wrong. It was the wrong kind of restaurant in the wrong street, in the wrong town, launched at the wrong time.' She got it right subsequently, though.

In the face of a lot of hostile criticism, we may need to bolster our self-belief. Even if you believe passionately and utterly in the potential of your idea, while the world seems not to, it always helps to have some outside endorsement. The best way to do this is to seek out people who do like your ideas and what you are trying to do. If you cannot find them, then it may be time to quit, and to move on to something else. This holds no fears for the creatively intelligent, because they know how to generate ideas. They have the attitude: 'ah well, I loved that idea, but, never mind, there are plenty more where that one came from'. As Walt Disney said when he was stitched up by businessman Charles Minx over his animated character Oswald, the Lucky Rabbit: 'Here – you can have the little bastard. You can have him – and good luck to you. Don't worry, there are plenty more characters where he came from.'

Watch Out For Experts

Experts concern themselves with 'what is', creators and entrepreneurs concern themselves with 'what might be'. No one would back Walt Disney to build Disneyland because they based their analysis on existing problems with theme parks: rides costly and insufficient, maintenance of a year-round park being expensive and a single entrance with standard entry fee being difficult to operate. But he knew that his vision would overcome all of these problems, and so he did it alone and, for the first time in his life, became securely solvent. James Dyson cites countless occasions where he was told: 'your idea can't be any good. If there was a better kind of vacuum cleaner, Hoover or Electrolux would have invented it.' But he knew otherwise.

Every response to your ideas is criticism; whether it is

ecstatically favourable or cruelly sneering. Without people responding, ideas become redundant. So, the more criticism you get, the more able you are to refine your ideas and make them highly successful. That is why you should grow addicted to it.

STAGE 12

The eureka programme: developing addiction to criticism

1. Take your pet idea of the moment and ask three people, whose opinion would be useful, to give you criticism. Accept their views, thank them for them and take away their criticisms and reflect on them.

2. Keep all of your positive criticism. Make a note of it if it is verbal, put it in a box file if it is written. This will be a valuable aid in developing a reality-checking addiction.

3. Give yourself a weekly fix of criticism by being sure to ask several people every week of their opinion of something you are involved in. Develop good critical friendships. And remember, you can reciprocate, if they would like you to.

So that's criticism dealt with – probably the biggest hurdle to making our ideas happen. But the coast is not entirely clear yet, I'm sorry to say; there are other little blighters lurking in our minds, which may make our progress difficult.

Dealing With Other Demons

This is the day Sally will start her novel. She has nothing in the diary, and a blank screen in front of her on the computer. Before she sits down to start writing, she feels the kitchen needs a clean. As she is cleaning the kitchen, she notices her cleaning supplies are running low, so she decides to pop to the shops. While she's there, she may as well buy some bathroom supplies too. On her return, with clean kitchen, new kitchen and bathroom supplies, she thinks she may as well give the bathroom a quick clean as well. It is now half past three, just half an hour before the children come home from school. Ah well, it doesn't look as though Sally will be starting her great work today . . .

Bill has taken the plunge, left his job and is now setting up his business. He has immersed himself in researching the matter: investigating different markets; ways of pricing; financial control; different types of wine; the logistics of holding wine-tasting parties in people's homes. He is loving it – and finding research very absorbing and different from the daily grind of the management job he held previously. The trouble is, he doesn't seem to know where to put boundaries on his research. With wine, for instance, Bill developed what he felt was a fairly good knowledge of French wines, and now he is tackling New World and Italian, a task that many would regard as a lifetime's work. Meanwhile, time is marching on . . . he has been researching for three months and has not yet been to see the bank manager.

Though Sally and Bill don't know it, there are little demons lurking in their minds, which are preventing them getting on and realising their ideas. Priorities and habits of thinking, which may have been useful in the past, no longer suit their current goals. This section is all about these habits and how to change them; with apologies to Pirandello, who wrote a play called *Six Characters in Search of an Author*, it really could be titled: *Six Demons in Search of a Creator*.

The Perfectionist Demon

This little blighter is obsessed with dotting every 'i' and crossing every 't' and it believes that perfection is possible and frequently desirable. You can often spot people who shelter this demon: they frequently are of neat and orderly appearance, with attention to detail and their behaviour will be well-controlled and orderly. Nothing wrong with any of this, but the Perfectionist Demon can prevent ideas getting off the ground by bogging its owner down in minor detail, and being far too ready to offer lots of negative criticism, keeping the idea firmly on the ground. Progress will be extremely slow and there will be little momentum because each stage of the idea has to be perfect before the creator can move on. Remember, this demon believes in perfection and anything short of this will come in for a savaging. So, if you are sitting there, neatly and tidily turning the pages of this book, then read on . . .

Tony is a filmmaker, who says:

I am a perfectionist and a pain to be with in many ways, because I like where I live and work to be very tidy, and I spend an obsessive amount of time getting my film to look the way I want it to. But I have realised too that this obsessive nature is what makes me good at film-making and gets my films commissioned and shown. So what I try and do to be a reasonable human being is to channel all my perfectionist tendencies into my work, and then try to take a more relaxed approach to other areas of my life.

And what about the perfectionist demon's love of noticing shortcomings? This is going to involve taking ideas apart and working out, in great detail, exactly what could go wrong with them. Perfectionism can stop ideas developing because of the risk of getting things wrong on the way. Many of the creative people I spoke to for this book said things like: 'I love having finished the first draft and then going back to revise it' or 'When I've done the entire rough form of the painting, and then I go back and refine it – that is what I really love doing.' It is improving as much as originating that brings them joy. The perfectionist demon needs to allow for the periods of chaos, hiatus and lack of resolve that the creative process involves. No one is marking your idea in the way that they would an answer to a test; they either want or need what you originate, or they don't.

So, with a perfectionist demon lurking inside your head, it is particularly important for you to immerse yourself completely in the vision of your idea, repeatedly asking yourself 'how could this be/work?' During this, that niggly critical voice has to be kept silent. When you've answered 'what do I need to do realise this?' about your vision, then you can allow the perfectionist demon a few words on what might go wrong.

Your Perfectionist Demon may have got into the habit of giving you globally condemnatory messages like 'you're a failure' or 'you've no imagination' or 'you're middle-aged and past it'. When it comes to creative intelligence, who we are is really rather irrelevant. There are lots of insecure, unbalanced, obsessive individuals who have been creatively productive and successful. So when your demon tries to tag you in this way, just remind them 'that's irrelevant'!

In workshops, we can always spot people harbouring Perfectionist Demons. They are always surprised and often confused by the positive feedback they get from others. Putting yourself in situations where you get as much feedback as possible, and listening and reflecting on this feedback, is one way of quieting this little demon. It also helps if the Perfectionist Demon realizes that we all have to create within limitations – of time, money and resources – and quite often we have to present work that is 'good enough'.

eureka!

STAGE 13

The eureka programme: dealing with perfectionism

1. Perfectionism often bogs down creators in small details so that they lose sight of the big picture in their schemes. It is vital, if you have perfectionist tendencies, that you stick to your deadlines, and identify and stick to one or two top priorities in making your idea happen. When the small stuff starts to distract you, remind yourself of the absolutely crucial goals that you must achieve within a timespan. Again, writing these down will help. Though a perfectionist may love order, ironically, their ideas may not happen because of a lack of structure and clarity about what the key essentials are.

2. Deadlines, however generous, can be problematic for the Perfectionist Demon. Any ideas need to be conceived of in terms of very clear priorities. For instance:

One month in: have plot finished/finance organised
    Two months in: have characters developed/wine ordered
    Three months in: chapter structure written, start writing/bookings in diary, lift off! When the allure of detail is then pulling too strongly, we can remind ourselves of overidding priorities that need attention.

The Serious Demon

During play, both humans and animals behave in particularly creative and flexible ways. We explore possibilities, make and destroy relationships, build things, work with rules and imitate, dramatise and use symbols. Play is full of imagination, metaphor and memories. The Serious Demon stops us playing. It makes us 100% adult, much concerned with analysis, reasoning and maturity. It ignores the face that our brains are wired to play, with circuits governing that function, and all the emotions like joy, laughter and camaraderie that go with it. The Serious Demon makes people earnest, and it may prevent you generating ideas, and expressing them to others. Deep down inside, you may feel that you are a lightweight, insignificant and unsubstantial.

People who take themselves seriously tend to seek out responsibility. They may get so burdened with looking after their workforce, their family and half the neighbourhood, that there is just no time for them to build their creative intelligence. They may have made life too burdensome for that. But hey, these people are forgetting something. To create is at the core of their being. To play is wired into their brains. They are being very grown-up, but only half-human. They need to get playing somewhere, somehow, with a messy hobby, hanging out with pleasure-seekers or taking up an extreme sport. They need to loaf around and watch some Woody Allen movies, or the entire series of 'The Office' or 'The Simpsons'.

People develop a strong Serious Demon because their identity is rather fragile and they dread the prospect of being laughed at by others. They love to apply common sense and reason to everything. But while common sense and reason have an important place in life, they are not what creative visions are about. Visions involve the imagination and suspension of rational disbelief. This involves projecting into the future and asking 'what if?' The Serious Demon rarely goes into the future, preferring to stick doggedly to the here and now, and 'what actually is'.

Humour is a highly creative activity because it involves the 'what might be' thinking of imagination and leaps of connection between thoughts. The Serious Demon concerns itself purely with 'what is' and can't leap to 'what might be' by putting two ideas from different contexts together. Below is how this works.

During the writing of this book, my car broke down and my husband and I waited for an AA man to come and repair it. When he arrived, this was how their dialogue went:

My husband: Is it ok if I go now? (leaving me with the car)

The AA man: Yes, don't worry, I'll look after her (i.e., me).

My husband: Yes, but will *she* look after you?

The AA man: It's a hazard of the job . . .

Somebody's dignity is usually the target of humour, and in this instance . . . I think it was mine.

So a Serious Demon lacks a sense of humour because it likes to progress in a linear, predictable, sensible fashion. It cannot make those leaps of connection that humour needs, and it does not understand the social role of humour as a way to endorse relationships. Ideas happen as a result of thoughts being connected through leaps of consciousness. They are useful, above all else, in how they relate to other people's experience. The Serious Demon can't think that way.

The Serious Demon can often stop you from expressing your ideas, because you fear taking the risk that others will not take you seriously. It spends a lot of its time protecting you from loss of face. Because exposing your ideas to others may mean that they take you less seriously, you never do this, and so those ideas never happen.

During my PhD research, several of the highly creative individuals I interviewed told me that a 'defining moment' for them was when they realised that other people's sneering didn't matter. It was an inevitable part of producing lots of ideas, and they might expect only 50% of these ideas to work anyway.

STAGE 14

The eureka programme: taking yourself less seriously

1. Learn something new or volunteer to do something silly that involves you dropping your defences and

risks making you look like a ninny. Remember that being open and learning are more important than your loss of face. Enjoy a feeling of freedom when this happens.

2. Hang out with people whose main purpose in getting together is to have a great laugh and enjoy themselves. Notice how making leaps of connection between disparate ideas work in humour, and experiment with a few yourself. You may not improve your creativity this way, but all those endorphins you are releasing will certainly boost your overall mood.

3. Give voice to whacky suggestions and shrug off others' disapproval. I can't emphasise enough how you need to learn to do this if you are going to earn a living in any way from being creative. Your ideas are just ideas. They exist outside of you and apart from you, and you are offering them to others to see if they strike chords. If people don't appreciate one of your ideas, then remind yourself that there are plenty more ideas where that one came from, or there will be by the time you have finished this book. And if people laugh at your ideas, congratulate yourself on having made them feel better for a short while.

The Self-Reverent Demon

Just recently, I've noticed an irritating little phrase that keeps creeping into conversation with some people: 'for me'. This is an interesting use of language, which sociolinguists might say reflects the ever-increasing individualism in our society. But, 'for me', this phrase is rather depressing. It tends to precede content that is aimed at showing just how unique and interesting that individual finds themselves to be. There is often an assumption made, too, that the rest of us are very happy to listen to someone's endless self-analysis. It reflects a failure on the part of the speaker to realise that, as human beings, we have far more in common with one another than we have differences.

The Self-Reverent Demon stops ideas from being realised, because the creator fails to appreciate that great ideas meet the needs, feelings and fantasies of others. The post-it note, the Filofax and the mobile phone are all ideas that help us function more efficiently, make us feel that we are better organised and more in control, and pander to those fantasies of being a super-effective mover and shaker. And scientific inventions, great art and literature will meet our needs, feelings and fantasies in different ways. Making ideas happen is all about connectivity, and self-centredness blocks that.

Many successful creators have had ideas, initially to meet their own needs, which they have then moulded to fit a market. Sarah Tremellen had great difficulty finding a generously sized bra when she first became a mother. So after some research, she realised that other women had this problem, too, and she started the mail-order company Bravissimo. Her business is now very successful, selling millions of pounds worth of bras every year. Sarah found there was gold in them there cups.

The Self-Reverent Demon can encourage us to behave in an indulgent, 'creative' manner, which ignores the truth that brilliant ideas transcend a single individual, and are much more significant than them.

Joely, a copywriter/art director in advertising, says:

When I first started in this business, I really thought I was uniquely talented and that my ideas showed me to be a highly strung thoroughbred amongst creatives . . . and I tried to behave a bit like that. I'd get fits of tempera-

ment and find it difficult to communicate with the clients when they were taking a conservative or penny-pinching approach. But when I looked at what was produced, I realised the best ads were the ones where we'd had really good communication – and that was what the work was about. The clients and other people in the agency couldn't care less about my dilemmas with the meaning of life – they just wanted me to come up with good ideas based on mutual understanding.

Earlier in this book, I described something called intra-personal intelligence, which is a high level of self-awareness. This requires some understanding of what motivates you, your strengths and weaknesses, and what you need and value in relationships. It involves understanding how you relate to others, and fit in, or otherwise, with them. The Self-Reverent Demon lacks this 'other' dimension – it is purely concerned with 'me, me, me'.

STAGE 15

The eureka programme: revering others

There is plenty of evidence for this kind of thinking in what are often called the creative industries. Television companies endlessly repeat reality TV formulas because they worked a couple of times; record companies constantly retry formulas for manufacturing pop groups like the Spice Girls; publishing companies repeatedly bring out the same type of book – easily categorizable as a result of a tried and tested formula (not this publisher and not this book, you understand).

No, to use your creative intelligence to produce ideas, you have to stick your neck out and risk criticism, and what may seem like personal rejection and controversy.

Tony, a managing director of a department store, where the business style is highly participative, explains it this way:

> When I first got the job, I used to get an idea, and then bring the subject up for discussion with my managers, getting their input on what direction we could take. I would hold back from expressing my idea, because I didn't want to be too directive and then spend a long time trying to get everyone on board with it. I soon learnt it was much more effective and more honest, actually, if I described my idea at the outset, then got their views on this. The discussion was much more focussed and productive. I suspect it's a matter of negotiating the role of being a leader – I was worried about appearing domineering and taking too many initiatives – in fact, my managers seem to expect that from me, and to quite like it, provided I listen and occasionally act on their views too!

Plagued by the Popularity Demon? Then you may be putting yourself under quite a lot of pressure. It's not easy sitting in silence in meetings when you are bursting with ideas, or seeing things work poorly when, if you spoke up, they could be a lot better. Plus, you owe it to yourself, don't you, to express your ideas? They are what make you unique, special and also able to contribute substantially to the benefit of others.

1. Avoid navel-contemplation and get out to do things with others; putting yourself into new and challenging environments is the best way to see yourself differently. Engaging in creative activity can make you feel better. The claims for creative writing being good therapy – and putting the bad stuff outside yourself – are considerable.

critical demons – and others

2. Go to places and events with the purpose of conducting research into other people. Talk to others to find out what makes them tick, how they live their lives and what they would like to have more or less of in them. Afterwards, reflect on what you have discovered and learnt.

3. Remember: 'By your results shall ye be judged!'

4. Remember, also you are not *that* interesting. Tussles you experience within your psyche are only interesting to others if a) they are being paid to psychoanalyse you, or b) they experience similar tussles themselves. What is interesting about you and your ideas are how they relate to everyone else.

The Popularity Demon

Now don't get me wrong – I'm not preaching war here – but realise that your ideas can be hampered by wanting to be liked, too much, and having too little thirst for battle. People who need a great deal of endorsement and encouragement from others, and who prefer to be part of a group much of the time, may not be cut out for creative challenges. Because of the ways our brains like to stick to tried and tested ruts of thinking, most people are inherently conservative. We like the familiar and the known, because it creates an illusion of stability. Whenever anyone comes along with a new idea, however brilliant that idea may seem, a part of us will be resisting, thinking that it threatens stability. Quite frequently, this thinking is unconscious.

STAGE 16

The eureka programme: caring less about popularity

1. Are you clear in your mind about what makes you unique? What are your most distinctive characteristics? And how do these work when you are in a group? This could be a work or family group; or group of friends. Are you comfortable being yourself or do you try too hard to fit in with other people's whims? Those of us who are overly concerned about popularity may have difficulties putting boundaries between ourselves and others – boundaries that announce 'this is who I am and this is what I think and feel'. We may need to rehearse statements about these matters aloud, before we announce them to others . . .

2. When you project an idea beyond yourself into the outside world, it gains collective ownership, rather like a memory, whether people agree with it or think it is totally potty. Your idea is the result of a particular conversation of neurons held in your head – and that's it. It is rarely a reflection of whether you are moral, kind or nice to children, cats and old ladies. But sensitivity and appropriateness are important, and you can factor that in – through how you intro-duce ideas. You can pre-empt possible adverse reactions with phrases like 'some of you may find this rather radical' . . . or 'this may not be the right time to suggest this . . . but . . .' or 'some of you may want to laugh at this idea', bearing in mind that people laughing at an idea may be no bad thing – at least your idea has caused an emotional reaction. Phrases like this will enable you to express your idea without feeling that you are running roughshod over other people's feelings.

3. For creativity to exist, there has to be destruction. Something must be destroyed and replaced with the new. So this demon must get the appetite for a spat. The more we depersonalise the battle, the better: this is a fight over a combination of thoughts, not over the creator's inadequacies. Fantasy alter-egos can be very helpful here; get a warrior queen or male equivalent character who sees off the Popularity Demon inside your head, and prevails when championing your ideas. I know that people get immensely frustrated when fear of conflict prevents them from expressing their ideas; often it helps to get used to speaking up and taking issue with things in routine meetings and discussions. The guideline here is that if you keep your behaviour relaxed and controlled, but speak very directly, then you are likely to get through much more effectively than if you grow angry or emotional and blur the message. Again, rehearse aloud, at home, beforehand. Worry the cat.

4. Because endorsement from others matters a great deal to the Popularity Demon, they may expect more encouraging feedback for their ideas than they can realistically expect to get. Just because you are not getting encouraging feedback for an idea, it doesn't mean it is no good. Remember those nine publishers that turned down J.K. Rowling.

The Novelty Demon

One of the most interesting questions about creative intelligence is why are some people so much more successful than others? I tried to answer this question by observing people I knew, and who I believed to be very creative. Why had one artist made himself a millionaire, while another, equally creative artist seemed barely able to make a living? Market considerations aside, what I discovered was that it seemed to be about how lateral or vertical their activities were. The millionaire artist had found one style of painting at which he excelled, was very popular and had pushed forward for years on this particular path. Some people in his situation would just repeat formulaically – not him, though. He kept pushing away at the boundaries of his particular style. His customers looked forward, consistently, to his next show. They knew what to expect – partially – but he also always managed to surprise them.

The less successful artist loved novelty. Most creative people do. It has been called 'germinational energy' – that buzz and excitement that new ideas and activities generate. The trouble is, this love of novelty had made his career a very tangential one. He'd painted a bit, sculpted a bit, written a bit, taught a bit, then got back to painting and was still dabbling in writing. Rather than Renaissance man, he was Renewing Man. Now, while there are notable individuals like Leonardo da Vinci who seem to be able to excel at everything they do, most creative people have a small number of activities at which they are very good. While this less successful artist had produced some marvellous work, he had never produced enough of it, or spent sufficient time and effort in marketing one style, to ever become successful. His love of novelty had prevented him fully realising his ideas, effectively.

In a time where our culture suffers from Attention Deficit Disorder, the Novelty Demon has a hold on a great many people. The media screams at us to buy new products, try new diets, read new books like this one . . . Being curious is part of creative intelligence, but to succeed, it needs to be focussed on a particular path. While lateral thinking – that is, thinking tangentially about issues – may be creative, too much lateral *activity* is not. Somewhere along the way, we have to decide 'this is what I find really interesting and this is now what will absorb my concentration and attention'. We have to ignore the extrinsic stimulant of novelty and concentrate on the intrinsic value of interest for its own sake.

STAGE 17

The eureka programme: curing novelty addiction

1. The Novelty Demon can be kept in its place by asking the question: 'Is this really new?' every time something novel attracts your attention. Whether you are in the role of researcher or consumer, often what you are being tempted by will be an old idea described in a new way. You want to avoid being distracted by something that is being superficially branded as 'new'. You don't want to kill this demon altogether; after all, interest in the new is the core of creative intelligence. However, you may want to ration the way it distracts you. Schedule half an hour daily, or an hour several times a week, where you unleash your Novelty Demon and it lets you surf the web, go window shopping, catch up on gossip or read newspapers and magazines.

2. Be aware that researching is getting input and you want to balance this with output in order to realise your idea. Are you clear about the core activities you need to perform to make your idea happen? Balance your love of novelty with a clear linear plan, with scheduled goals and mini-goals en route, as described in the last chapter. Stare long and hard at this line if you sense your novelty addiction resurfacing, and get back to activity that helps you move along it.

The Time Demon

In Chapter Three, I talked about the very important role of the unconscious in creative intelligence and how it has at least two different speeds of operating. The Time Demon doesn't understand this. It wants ideas and it wants them fast and, in imposing frequent and predictable deadlines, it kills ideas before they are born. Unlike the Perfectionist Demon, who thinks attention to detail equals effective, the Time Demon believes effectiveness means rapid and frequent delivery.

Because of the tendency of our brains to think in engrained and uncreative patterns, having too much routine in our schedules will amplify this tendency. So, while we all need deadlines – and some people are brilliantly creative when up against them – too many regular deadlines are likely to turn the brain into complacent traditional IQ mode, rather than a creatively intelligent one. A head of research at a science establishment came on one of my workshops, and his remit was to get his team of research scientists to come up with 'four great ideas every month'. It would have been wiser had the brief been 'forty to fifty ideas every year'. First of all, the scientists could experiment with varying time scales for their idea-generating, and, secondly, they would feel much more motivated having choice over their own timescales. This way, the everyday rut and routine would be avoided.

Annette is a marketing expert who says:

I went on a workshop where I was identified as a 'hurry-up' type of personality. These are people who apparently thrive on lots of last-minute activity and can then produce excellent work under this pressure – but of course make it difficult for other people they may have to work with who don't share this love of adrenalin. In truth I realised it makes me feel important and powerful to be rushing

*like mad close to deadlines – and, although often my last-
minute panicking is rather showy, I will have done most
of the ground work. It's almost as though I'm testing the
nerve of the people who work for me – and not very fair.
I realised too that it only happens four or five times a year
– at the end of projects of varying lengths of time – if it
was happening more regularly, I suspect the team and I
would have burnout. I have had to acknowledge that
working like this makes me feel smarter than everyone else
– but that I am not getting the best out of them, and our
results might be even better, if I was more considerate.*

STAGE 18

The eureka programme: resisting time pressure

1. 'Busyitis', the cult of being busy, which is epidemic
   today, is about being wanted. When we have full
   diaries, psions or palm pilots crowded with appoint-
   ments, we feel that other people need us. If the Time
   Demon has got you in his evil grip, it may be time to
   decide 'what's more important – being wanted, or
   creating what I want to?' To create, your unconscious has to be able to mill over ideas and chuck
   them back and forth into your conscious mind; they
   need to trail gently around those circuits in your
   head . . . and for that, you need drift-time.

2. As much as you are able to, avoid routine. If your job
   involves lots of predictable repetition, then organise
   your out-of-work time to minimize this. Try and get
   periods of time, two or three hours at a stretch,
   where you have nothing scheduled. Now, as a
   working mum with a young family, I know this can be
   difficult. But it may be worth putting in extra hours

over a few long days, to free up these periods. Trade swop-periods with your partner or others in a similar situation to your own.

3. Curb the urge to be a martyr, feeling that you should be constantly busy, either on work matters or on the efficient running of the home. Only lions love 'em – martyrs, that is. When the idea of pottering about for a few hours, not really doing much, is too indulgent to contemplate, then just do something different in these periods. And there are lots of ways of getting 'creative time' where you can take the family out and still get out of the rut – a visit to a beach in winter, say, or an outing to a museum or place of historical interest. You just want to go into a slightly different world, where constant time deadlines do not prevail. Pixar animated movies, like *Finding Nemo*, *Monsters Inc* and *Buzz Lightyear* are always a good bet in bad weather, whatever your age or preferences.

People who talk a lot about their ideas but never realise them are people who are not receiving criticism usefully. At any time during the creative process, you may find it useful to get some critical feedback. You will certainly want to get some when you have formed your vision, and again when you are selling your ideas. When you get stuck, you may want to obtain criticism in order to take a different approach. It can prevent you from spending a lot of time and energy going in the wrong direction.

Of course, after you've taken on board criticism and dealt with your demons, you will find yourself once more needing to generate ideas. This chapter has been all about your playing the role of researcher; now let's turn to the other vital aspect of making ideas happen: that of being a builder of creative ideas. And to build on Chapter Three about your unconscious potential, we will now look at conscious thinking techniques for idea-generation.

6

Soft in the Head

Believing — Immersing — Idea generating — Creating a Vision — Reality-checking — Piloting — Realising

This chapter is about more idea-generating.

Just imagine you are a brain. Life's not that easy for most brains. There is a complicated world out there to negotiate, complex relationships to develop, you're under siege from ever-increasing media and technological stimulation. You do what brains are good at: help their owner survive through categorising stimuli, then organising and filing them in a logical, orderly way. You create patterns of recognition for your owner. So when your owner is presented with new information or stimuli that they have never encountered before, your neatly ordered pattern-system sorts out how what they are experiencing in the *present* matches what they have encountered in the *past*.

But, now, brain, I want you to think . . . is your organising and retrieving always that helpful? Are there times when your categorising and organising results in limiting your owner's options? Is it possible that your love of neat analysis is not always appropriate for a world that can be extremely messy?

Yes, brain, you've got it. Those habits of categorising and ordering can get you stuck in a rut or a groove. In the many circumstances that require creative intelligence, you need to break out of these hard, engrained patterns. Circumstances do not repeat themselves identically, and, while rapidly categorising and ordering may create an impression of stability, these habits may be inappropriate for new situations where elements of uncertainty reside. The categorical, hard thinking of traditional IQ has its limits, putting you, brain, on a fixed path. What you need to do, oh brain, is to talk to your owner. You need to urge them to get soft in the head.

This chapter will show them how.

We have already considered the role of the unconscious in generating ideas in Chapter Three. Now we look at how we can use conscious creative thinking techniques to generate ideas. Knowing these techniques is extremely helpful, because, when something blocks your ideas from coming to fruition – a lack of money or disappointing market reponse, perhaps – then you can shrug your shoulders philosophically and go, 'Well there are plenty more where that one came from'. It is usually people who lack confidence in their ability to idea-generate who are paranoid about idea protection . . . unless they are lawyers profiting from the activity!

You may need to idea-generate anywhere within the creative process. You will have had ideas before creating your vision, but when your vision is aired or manifested in reality, then the critical response to it may have you rushing back to the idea-generating drawing board. Similarly, when you start piloting and selling your ideas and involving others in their realisation, then you will need to keep generating ideas. This has to be *the* core CQ skill.

Hard in the Head

Workshops and research have convinced me that we can all learn to think with creative intelligence. Through becoming aware of the patterns our brains naturally prefer – their default settings, if you like – and learning other ways of thinking, adults and children can dramatically increase their capacity for creating and learning. In a perfect world, every school in the land would have thinking studies as a vital part – indeed, at the core – of their curriculum. But our world is not perfect, so, as a step in the right direction, here is how you, and those you influence, can think more creatively. This chapter contains a creative thinking 'make over': a whole range of techniques that can be used in all sorts of contexts.

But first I want to tackle the question: why do we become rigid, categorical and inflexible in how we think?

Our brains are wired so that we can quickly and easily make sense of the environment. They connect stimulants with appropriate responses. We see a road sign saying 'stop' and we know it would be nuts to drive on. We smell burning and we know we need to go and check that pizza we forgot about in the oven. We hear a fire engine pulling up very close to us, and we rush outside to check the property of the forgetful lady next door. Quick responses help us handle potential danger, and to survive. But they also help us misjudge, because we can fall into the trap of making assumptions when we make these quick connections. Using categories and associations that already exist in our brains, we infer and make meaning from them. A couple of years ago, you may have seen a recruitment campaign for the police force in the UK, which exploited this. The advert showed a black man and a white man having a fight, and we were urged to guess which one was the police officer. The copywriters knew that the vast majority of people in this country would immediately assume that the white man was the police officer. It is hardly surprising, then, that we see evidence of hard, simplistic, over-categorical thinking in social groups whose members feel insecure and have low status. Note the white nationalism in deprived sink estates, and hatred of sex offenders in prisons.

But it's not just security that limits our thinking potential it is also a need for stability. We categorise things quickly, according to our previous experience, in order to make us feel relatively stable. Notice the difference between the feelings generated when we meet someone who says she is doctor, has a kindly, motherly air and listens attentively to us, and the feelings generated when we meet someone of indeterminate gender who says they are a genetic engineer, and has an upper class accent and multiple piercings and tattoos. In the first instance, the great majority of us would feel comfortable quite quickly; in the second, the great majority of us would feel confused. The genetic engineer just wouldn't 'add up'. The motherly doctor would be placed on our sense-making maps quickly and easily, and would make us feel stable. The need to have to investigate further the identity of the genetic engineer might make quite a lot of us feel uncomfortable.

Feeling insecure and slightly unstable is part of developing CQ. The three roles of creative intelligence – playing builder or creator, researcher and critic or evaluator – all require us to ask questions and to confront the answers honestly, whether we like them or not. No questions asked – no creative intelligence; it is as simple as that. A creative intelligence mantra could be 'Don't assume. Question'. Our urge to create and achieve must take precedence over our need for security and stability *in certain areas of our lives*. It is quite possible, also, that the urge to create and achieve can distract from and help us cope with unhappiness in other areas of our lives. A number of exceptional creators have described unhappy childhoods, where what they created became a distraction from the horrors of reality. Anthony Trollope, inventor of the post-box and prolific nineteenth-century novelist, described his childhood in his autobiography thus:

As a boy, even as a child, I was thrown much upon myself. I have explained, when speaking of my school-days, how it came to pass that other boys would not play with me. I was therefore alone, and had to form my plays within myself. Play of some kind was necessary to me then, as it has always been. Study was not my bent, and I could not please myself by being all idle. Thus it came to pass that I was always going about with some castle in the air firmly built within my mind.

There can, I imagine, hardly be a more dangerous mental practice; but I have often doubted whether, had it not been my practice, I should ever have written a novel. I learned in this way to maintain an interest in a fictitious story, to dwell on a work created by my own imagination, and to live in a world altogether outside the world of my own material life.

STAGE 19
The eureka programme: embracing uncertainty

1. Where worrying is stopping you from accepting uncertainty and instability, you could try the following. Talk about your worries to other people and send yourself up, Woody Allen-style, for being so neurotic. Read Jonathon Franzen's much-acclaimed novel *The Corrections* to laugh at a fabulously neurotic central character. Personify this worrying tendency as a gremlin or demon and create fantasy scenarios where it shrinks into oblivion or gets shot or mowed down by a tank, which represents your hugely opti-

mistic vision. And finally, compartmentalise your worrying and insecurity by giving yourself a thirty-minute slot where you do nothing else but worry! Then get on with life . . .

2. Your creative endeavours may involve uncertainty in your work-life or leisure time. But much in your life will remain stable and predictable. Research shows that human beings generally dramatise the predicted effects of change far more than actually occurs. A mental image of yourself as a hunter, explorer, chancer or genius scientist may help. Create a role for yourself in your mind, where you are out in the world, living by your wits and relishing every challenge that comes your way. Discover your inner Ellen MacArthur or Richard Branson, imagining you are opportunistically thriving in an unpredictable environment.

3. Where what you have embarked upon has completely thrown out a routine, create some sort of regularity. Gym visits, coffee with friends or just a daily walk can help create feelings of stability in some areas of life, and will compensate for the exciting roller coaster ride you have embarked on in others.

4. Give ballast mentally to the areas of your life where you do have some stability. If feelings of anxiety about an unpredictable project are threatening to overwhelm you, take some time out and think about areas of your life that make you feel stable and secure – relationships, favourite places you go to, meetings with friends, hobbies. Make more of them, if necessary.

5. The most successful people are plagued by bouts of self-doubt and uncertainty, but do not necessarily reveal them in public. Fear and uncertainty may be relegated to their proper place – as a resource to help us question things periodically – by ensuring that you have a strong sense of vision and goals, as described in Chapter Four.

Constructing Reality

The brain works as a self-organising system; it likes patterns, lines and sequences. It likes to categorise and put things in alignment, and constantly sorts information and stimulus through sense-making activities. One of our most basic sense-making activities is about how things are similar and how they are different.

Let me take you back to babyhood for a moment. As babies, one of the very first things we understand is that feeling hungry is different from feeling well-fed. Where both parents are present, babies will work out that their mother is different from their father. When parents are lucky, their babies may work out quite early on, that day is different from night. But, back to adulthood and how these similarities and differences operate in everyday life, where your patterns say: 'bookshops = exciting' and 'clothes shops = irrelevant' as you walk down a high street, so that you will know where to go. If your patterns say 'tall dark handsome men = nice' and 'small bespectacled ones = dull', you will know who to talk to. If they say 'vegetables = good and healthy' and 'white sugar = deadly', you will know what to buy. These patterns seek to keep you feeling stable, but, in doing so, they can also very literally, get you into a rut.

At the risk of sounding overly philosophical here, to know what something is, you must know what it is not. So these comparisons, or constructs, are the way you filter your experiences and make sense of the world. They are metaphorical chopsticks in your mind, with one value at one end, and the opposite in meaning to you at the other end. You probably have hundreds or even thousands of them floating around. Many of your constructs will be common to other people: constructs we all have in common, for instance, are – good . . . bad; similar . . . different; masculine . . . feminine; right . . . wrong; superior . . . inferior. But the particular combination of constructs and their relative significance are likely to be unique to each of us, based as they are on a combination of genetic and conditioning influences.

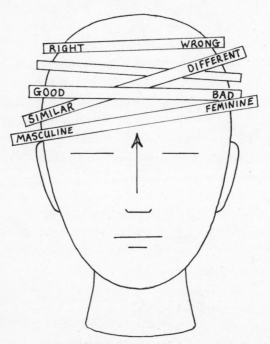

The most practically accessible way of using constructs is to convert them into questions. Let's say one of your important constructs is self-development and that the opposite of that, to you, would be stagnation. You frequently convert this construct into the question: 'what opportunities are presented here for development and growth?' – especially at work.

You now have a meeting with a departmental manager whose most frequently used construct is cynicism, a very defensive position. He sees the opposite of cynicism as naivete and foolishness. He converts this construct into the question 'what evidence can I find of naïve optimism in this situation?' You and he are meeting to discuss a potential training programme – and yes, you would be right to think that communication could be difficult at the outset. For your communication with him to work properly, you would need to establish some constructs in question form that you hold in common. These could be questions like 'what can we do to make our business more successful?'

All of your ideas will be based on constructs, and they involve both conscious and unconscious thinking. When people are asked on workshops to identify constructs that are important to them, they often find it easy to identify something they know they value, but find it difficult to describe its opposite, possibly because what is negative may lurk more deeply in the unconscious. Let me give you an example:

Sally was asked how she felt when she was making an idea happen. She said 'exhilarated, powerful and effective'. Then she was asked what the opposite of these feelings was to her. She found this much more difficult to articulate. She finally said 'bored, tired, disengaged'. Quite understandably, she didn't want to feel like this often, so she was not keeping it readily available in her conscious mind.

Constructs are not restricted to verbal descriptions; they include ideas that may be better visualised, heard or even felt. The gentle stroking of your hand contrasted with the embedding of sharp nails into your flesh would create a construct. Anne Sullivan understood this when she taught the blind, dumb and deaf Helen Keller, via a brilliant idea she had. She wet her finger and wrote the letters for the word 'water' repeatedly on Helen's palm. Eventually, Helen Keller came to understand that Anne Sullivan was describing the water and they had a means of communication. Anne Sullivan used the construct 'available senses contrasted with unavailable senses' to ask the question: what sense does Helen have available?

STAGE 20

The eureka programme: constructs you like

1. Take your mind back to a time where you have made an idea work and recall how you felt then. Perhaps you had several feelings. Write down each feeling and then work out what its opposite meaning is for you. Do not worry about your powers of articulacy here. Having the totally apposite word is not important; what matters is that you convey satisfactorily to yourself what the feeling was. Now turn these constructs into questions that you ask yourself as you seek to realise your ideas.

When Carl did this exercise, he said:

A few years ago, I had an idea for a stage act that I wanted to do with some friends: a sort of spoof hypnotism act called 'The Fabulous Mesmerists'. I asked a couple of friends I rather admired to join me, and they did. We worked on our act and became rather a cult success on the university and college circuit. I will never forget the feelings I had when we first started rehearsing. As constructs, they would be:

Huge feeling of achievement vs. dull, risk-free exis-

tence. Disbelief I was working with such great people vs. I should expect good fortune. Exhilaration vs. mild depression.

This was all when I was a student. But my job now involves getting teams of really good people together to develop new products – and I am very much motivated by questions like: 'can we achieve something amazing here?', 'where are the best people do to this?' and 'am I keeping this project dynamic or is it stagnating?'

Activating Constructs

We can activate constructs so that they shape the way we interpret the world. Successful entrepreneurs always have a strong 'looking for opportunity . . . not nothing doing here' construct, which translates into the question: 'are there any opportunities in this situation for me?' – which is active much of the time for them. In earlier chapters, as part of the eureka programme, I have suggested that you get out your antennae and pay particular attention to certain things in the environment, like, for instance, products of creative intelligence. Entrepreneurs see more opportunities than other people because this construct is one that is so active for them.

You will almost certainly have had experience of this, perhaps with less pleasant matters. A tax bill arrives in the post and, the rest of the week, you hear other people talking about tax matters, see articles on tax in the papers and hear items on the radio about tax. Unless it a special time of the year for tax collection, then objective reality hasn't changed. It's just that you have activated a 'paying tax' construct that is getting your antenna twitching every time you hear mention of the idea in objective reality. In the same way, if you have worked out very carefully what your pet idea involves, those constructs will be activated and you will find more opportunities to act on them.

Creative Tension

You may well be sensing here that there is a danger, when we talk about using constructs, of doing over-simplistic, black-and-white, either/or, thinking. And you'd be right. This is seeing the world in parallel lines, and, since the end of the Roman dominance in European history, this has been a dangerously limited perspective. While parallel lines make everything seem ordered and controlled, it is not really how the world is. When we are over-categorical about people, problems or decisions being either bad or good, right or wrong, difficult or easy, we make our world seem less complicated, and easier, apparently, to control. But most individual people are rarely entirely bad or good; they are good in some circumstances, bad in others, and a lot of them will just be muddling along in a typically human way, being neither particularly one way or the other.

So, while constructs are a useful way of describing how we very basically make sense of things, they can also be very limiting. We can get ourselves stuck between one end of a construct and the other, and keep vacillating between the two. We can get stuck in a rut in our thinking, so that we see ourselves as having very limited choices. The most common limiting construct people hold about their creativity is that of:

My job . . . opportunity to be really creative.

And they view themselves as being totally trapped by their job – in a non-creative state. Now, undoubtedly, a lot of jobs do lack creative potential, but there are all those hours you don't work, and there may be opportunities to go to a more creative role within the organisation. So, rather than getting stuck between these opposing ideas, a creative approach is to move to a third, new idea, like a creative project after-hours. This is thinking triangularly, if you like, so that, rather than getting stuck between two contrasts, you move to a third place.

Studies of highly creative people and effective leaders frequently show that they have a higher tolerance for triangular solutions, and that if they are being wrenched from one end to the other of a construct, rather than quickly acting to ease the conflict, they learn to live with it, tolerate it, and build something new in order to deal with it. In many different contexts, this has been described as 'tolerance of ambiguity', 'paradox', 'ambivalence', 'dichotomy' or 'dialectic'. In politics, it is sometimes described as 'the third way'. Richard Rothenberg, a researcher, believes that this ability to tolerate contradiction is at the heart of creative intelligence, and he calls it Janusiun thinking, after Janus, the two-faced Roman god.

Creative tension, then, is a useful impetus to moving to a third, or even fourth or fifth, place. In making that move, we can generate brilliant ideas.

STAGE 21

The eureka programme: two-faced thinking

1. Can you identify the constructs that make your idea contract? Here are some contradictory constructs about modern family life:

   Parents want kids to enjoy free time . . . parents often are tired themselves. Parents want to relax themselves during holidays . . . but have to entertain the children. Earning money exhausts parents . . . but it doesn't buy them energy. Disneyland, kids' camps and hotels with extensive childcare all go some way to easing these contradictions.
   Pret a Manger, the fresh fast food business,

recognised the contradiction that office workers want quick lunches they can grab on-the-run, but that they also want fresh, tasty food that does them good. Johnny Boden, owner of Boden, the catalogue clothing company, recognised that middle-class people want middle-priced, good-quality clothes, but that they don't have time to shop for them – and that a lot of these people are city-dwellers who like to imagine they live in the country.

Behind this book, for instance, is the tension in the construct:

Innately, we want to express and realise our ideas . . . this urge has to compete with many other demands in our lives.

When you are looking to develop a new idea, look around your subject area and your environment, and ask yourself, where are the contradictions here? (This is also a good approach to identifying rich areas for research – in any subject under the sun.)

2. Feeling stuck while working on an idea? Identify what different directions you feel you are being pulled in, what the contradictions are that you are experiencing, then see if you can move your idea forward to some third place or position, which will give you new impetus.

Creative Mind-play

The following techniques will help you build CQ, and generate more and more ideas. Remember that every time you use a new way of thinking, you rewire your brain slightly so that it becomes more effective. Practising these techniques is a great way of developing a creative mindset when you are stuck in a queue at the supermarket or on slow-moving public transport. The idea is to develop a creative mindset, rather than use a specific creative thinking technique at a particular time, to make your brilliant ideas happen. The aim of this is to develop your potential so that you have an endless supply of brilliant ideas.

To make these techniques as practically useful as they can be, I have described how Bill, an aspiring entrepreneur, and Sally, an aspiring novelist, could use them in real life.

Seeing spiders

Psychologists often describe thought processes as 'convergent' or 'divergent'. Convergent thinking proceeds logically and in a linear fashion towards a clear final goal. A convergent thought process would involve a step-by-step approach, categorising things, eliminating side issues and moving towards closure. Were Sally to approach her novel this way, she might decide to write about something she knows about – the academic world, for instance – ignoring any associative ideas arising outside her knowledge area, and plotting her novel stage by stage, as a journey of the central character. Bill might decide to base his business on skills he already has, giving himself definite goals over the next year, according to where he will be, and planning his progress in a linear fashion.

Divergent thinking proceeds laterally – jumping in different directions, and entertaining possibilities. A divergent thought process involves making leaps away from your point of origin, and seeing where these leaps take you, in a random fashion. This is the process described as mind-mapping, where a central idea is planted in the middle of a blank sheet of paper and other associations that spring to mind are written and drawn as symbols around the central idea. Then links are created between all the ideas. So, were Sally to approach her novel writing this way, she might stick a picture of a book in the middle of a page, and then generate possibilities around it, that are just anything to do with the central idea. Bill might decide to take an 'experience mapping' trip, where he visits loads of different businesses and start-up agencies, just to get the feel of the terrain.

The key difference between these two approaches is that the first is linear, and the second is web-like. The first converges on the end goal, and in doing so eliminates what seem to be side issues, fairly swiftly. The second is much more exploratory, includes all sorts of possibilities, and takes place in a far more meandering fashion. Most of us are very comfortable and well-trained in using the first approach; it is the second one that is more demanding. And it is the second one that distinguishes creative intelligence. So I am urging you to think about your subject area, and the environment in which you operate, as a spider's web, full of divergent possibilities – that is, a network of connections. This is a vital skill in making ideas happen because, when you see your world as web, with a number of interconnecting systems, dynamic and fluid in character, it is much closer to how the world actually works, and you are looking at your idea in a way that mirrors the real world more effect-ively. Your idea is being conceived of in a manner that makes it suit real life better. But when you view your idea as a neat furrow, along which you push a productive plough, then you are producing a predictable, linear concept that might meet approval from a small number of extreme control-freaks, but that's all!

Where Sally and Bill use both these approaches, they will use their minds to create spiderwebs and plough furrows. Sally will locate her experiences of working in a university library at the centre of her web, and consider all the possible surrounding settings for this world, and who would be in them and how they would interact with the central characters. But her story will have a linear sense too, in following the central character's story. Bill will gather lots of market intelligence in a web-like fashion to locate what he wants to do, but he will plan strategy and goals for himself in a linear manner.

When ideas come to fruition, and become popular, it is always because someone, somewhere, will have looked at how the idea fits into the web of the world, or a particular market-place. It is essential to do this big-picture thinking, or your creative intelligence may remain undiscovered. The question that smart spider-thinkers constantly ask is: 'How does this idea fit in with its environment, and how does it link to other environments?'

As a final thought for this section, are you aware of what spiders do when their webs are destroyed? They build bigger, more complex and more beautiful ones. There's a good metaphor for life, if I ever met one.

STAGE 22

The eureka programme: Spider-minding

1. If you have never used this technique before, you
   may find it helpful to draw a spider's web of your life,

with pictures of all its different elements and how they are linked. Don't rush this, muse over it, and note how many elements unexpectedly link with one another. You may find it useful to do this with a partner or friend and to do a 'what do you find interesting about this?' analysis afterwards, showing each other your creations.

2. Take your idea and put that at the centre of a spider's web, too. Again, draw around it everything that seems relevant in the environment in which you operate and mull it over making links between things. Are there gaps that could be filled? Do you really know about your environment or do you need to do more research? Would it be useful to show this to someone who knows a lot about your chosen area of expertise, and to ask them for input on it?

3. Any time you get stuck on the way to making your idea happen, stop and draw a web of where you are with it. Surround it with other ideas and their webs, too. Solutions present themselves this way. They are not always short-term ones, though. Charlie came on one of my workshops and said:

I was trying to introduce this new service at work, and I drew the idea with a surrounding web, and then drew all the other new things people were trying to introduce. I realised my idea was tiny and rather hopeless by comparison – I could either leave the company and go elsewhere to try and implement it – or destroy it, stay put and start spinning something new that would be regarded as being much more significant.

Zooming in and out

You don't need a canvas chair that says director on the back to use this technique, but you are, in effect, playing around with an imaginary film camera.

Building on this idea of your operating inside a spider web, or interconnecting system, creative thinking involves playing with a zoom lens, and honing in on your idea or project, to either make it very small and specific, or much bigger and all-encompassing. What happens if you shrink your thinking and come in really close up, or expand it and go for a wide panorama? For Sally, this would be the difference between a narrow focus on the rarefied nineteenth-century world of a Jane Austen novel, or the broad sprawl of something by Tom Wolfe or Balzac. In Bill's case, where he is thinking of starting a wine delivery and tasting business, it would be a choice between focussing on a small upmarket geographical area with a discerning selection of fine wine or going for a much wider catchment area and supplying plonk for all pockets. You probably realise there could be all sorts of permutations here. Sally could make her novel sprawl in time, but focus in tiny on a family or small group of people. Bill could develop a wide delivery area, geographically, but still concentrate on upmarket customers. The key is to think of your mind as working like that of a film director or a kaleidoscope.

Edward de Bono has written a great deal about creative thinking and one of the techniques he prescribes is called 'focussing' – which is concentrating for an unusual amount of time on a small area of your subject matter. This would mean coming in for a close-up shot and lingering there for a good while. It is during this lingering and focussed attention that the leaps of connection between thoughts, which form great ideas, can arise.

This is an amazingly simple approach and merely requires you to fix your attention on a particular area or subject for a period of time. I suspect that this may be the key for many people in building their creative intelligence – that they just take time to stop and look and absorb, rather than rush off to analyse and act.

STAGE 23

The eureka programme: zooming

1. Choose something very specific about your idea that interests you. Create a project of zooming in close to something and investigating it very thoroughly. Then work out which aspects of it could be generalized to make a much bigger picture and zoom out. Put it into a big panoramic sweep of subjects, which could include the entire field you are working in, or a specific geographical area, or even the whole world.

2. Zooming can be very practical indeed; it is the observing part of playing the role of researcher. Bill could go to wine-tastings and observe in great detail, for instance, how people behave, and what motivates them there. Try going somewhere and intensely observing some practical aspect of your idea.

Different worlds, different viewpoints

In *Weird Ideas That Work*, Robert Sutton describes some research by Gary Hamel, a well-known American academic, into Marks and Spencer:

There is a Marks & Spencer food store in most English towns of any size. When the company got into the sand-wich business a few years ago, they realised it was a massively inefficient process. In particular, the English like sandwiches with butter, which means that, every day,

*people in sandwich shops throughout the country spread
soft butter on bread slices by hand. Martin von
Zwanenberg, then Marks & Spencer's head of Home
Services and Technology, realised that 'if we wanted to
expand, this was unacceptable – we'd have to have
everyone in the company buttering bread'. A few days later,
von Zwanenberg visited a supplier who made bed sheets
for Marks & Spencer and noticed they were using a silk-
screen process to print patterns. He tried an experiment:
'We filled up one of the ink vats with butter and screen-
printed butter onto cotton'. Marks & Spencer now silk-
screens butter onto bread, which is one reason why it is
now a major player in the sandwich business in England.*

This illustration is a fine example of someone having a
problem in one context, and then making a creative leap of
connection in another context. It's like the design engineer
who, faced with the challenge of coming up with a revolutionary bridge design, went into the different world of the
human body, and took as his starting point the question, 'What
makes the perfect human handshake?' The connections work
through having one preoccupation hanging around slowly
simmering on the back-burner – probably in the unconscious
– while in the other context our conscious mind is asking 'how
do things work in this world then' and 'what happens in this
location?' So Sally, the budding authoress, might research a
different world to the one of academia – say, museums or
hospitals – to find interesting and inspiring similarities and
differences for her novel. It could occur to Bill that cosmetics,
books, Tupperware and sex toys have all been sold through
house parties; perhaps the time has come to do the same with
wine . . .

Another way of playing this game is to imagine different
people are looking at your area of interest. You take different

perspectives and imagine what those people's concerns and interests would be. So Sally might imagine the perspectives of a literary agent, a commissioning editor and a typical book buyer. Bill might imagine what Avon Cosmetics and Ann Summers customers might want from a wine-tasting party. The mind boggles at all the possibilities.

Einstein developed the theory of relativity by imagining a subject from different perspectives. We can put two techniques together here usefully by mapping relevant people on a spider web around a subject in the middle, and then considering and imagining how those people would view the subject from their particular vantage point.

STAGE 24

The eureka programme: different but similar

1. Deliberately experience a different world through a book or visit somewhere, talking to someone in depth about a world that is quite different from your own. When you get back home and have some reflection time, consider what parallels and connections there are between that world and your own area of interest. Is there something that works especially well in the different world, which you use in your own? It's vital that you don't have the sense of 'I am taking my idea to this different world'. You should reflect on the world you have experienced, and its strengths, and then take a fresh look at your idea. Museums, historical buildings, art galleries, farm parks and science centres are all very stimulating. Some of us might even suggest Selfridges fits the bill, too.

2. Take your project and choose three different types of people with different world views – a scientist or

artist, perhaps, a religious leader, a left or right wing politician, a business leader, a teacher or a social worker. Think in depth about how they would regard your project, what they would identify with in it and what would alienate them. Don't feel that you need change your project in order to please everyone; this is an exercise to help you gain fresh perspectives, which often result in clarifying and strengthening your existing position.

Being Subversive

Creative intelligence involves challenging 'givens', asking the right questions, querying why something is a problem rather than accepting things as stated. It is about breaking norms, moulds and boundaries and reinventing something in their place. Creativity is one end of a construct, and most people would suggest that the opposite of creativity is destruction. One cannot exist without knowing the other.

Being subversive involves challenging, spunky behaviour. As one inventor commented, 'I constantly ask myself, "Hey, what sucks around here?" Then I know I am looking at an area that has potential for invention.' When confronted with a problem, creative people ask: 'why is this a problem?', 'whose cause does it serve for it to be a problem?' and 'does it have to be resolved or can it be ignored or circumvented?' They also tend to ask similar questions about rules, like: 'why is this a rule? 'whose cause does it serve?' and 'does it have to be obeyed, or can it be ignored, circumvented or even flagrantly trounced?' Problems and rules involve boundaries, and creative intelligence pushes at these to see whether they can be broken and redrawn. One of the most frequent questions asked by the creatively intelligent is 'how can I interpret this differently?' So Sally's novel, about salacious academics and raunchy librarians, might expose the dark underbelly of university life and Bill's wine party planners, with their 'guess the wine' games, would undermine the idea that wine-tasting is rarefied, and only for the rich and cultured.

Product inventors deliberately examine rules about products and question them when they are trying to come up with something new. So they would take something like 'hair shampoo' and describe its qualities. The first quality could be liquid. They might then ask, 'does it need to be liquid; could it be solid, like shoe polish in a can, or soap?' Just asking that question might result in the creation of a new, solid, travel shampoo. A few years ago, a product inventor queried the rules about chocolates, and came up with the rule that they should be served at room temperature. 'Why?' queried the developer, and now it is possible to buy our favourite chocs made into frozen versions, so we can enjoy them all year round.

STAGE 25

The eureka programme: subversion

1. Confront the sacred cows and traditions in the area where you are working. Why do they exist and have they outserved their use? If someone is blocking your idea because of 'rules', keep asking as many people as you need to: 'what is the purpose of this rule, and, if it serves nothing, please could we change it?' I realize that, in many situations, this may require dogged determination and even a lengthy lobbying campaign.

2. Whenever you get a wild idea or subversive fantasy, ask yourself 'what tension does this ease?' to deduce whether it is a goer. You don't have to feel this tension to identify it. Talking to others can verify your

suspicions. Remember, you need not identify a problem to come up with a great idea; the problem can be identified later.

Asking What If?

To generate ideas and create scenarios, it is very useful to ask the question 'what if?' Sally will build twists and turns into her plot through asking 'what if?' several times over the scope of her story. Bill might ask 'what if people would like cheese or olives or canapés supplied with their wine?' or 'what if people join my wine club to buy in bulk at considerable discount?' or 'what if . . . I supply interesting cordials, smoothies and juices for the non-drinkers at my wine-tasting parties?' in order to think of ways of extending his business.

Several years ago, a retail client of mine was finding it hard to get and keep good staff. Retail hours were getting longer and longer, and finding people who wanted to spend long periods of time on the shop floor, in an area of high employment, was proving difficult, despite the business's excellent reputation. The HR Director asked the question, 'What if the norm in this business became that almost everyone works part-time?' They introduced this idea and now have a well-established workforce, 80% of whom work part-time, which includes many happy parents who have enjoyable work and time to spend with their families.

Random linking games can sometimes help with shaking up perspectives on ideas. Let's say Bill took a random word like 'shed' and tried to link it back to his business idea. The leaps could go 'shed' to 'garden' to 'summer' to 'seasonal parties' to 'barbecue wine-tastings'.

STAGE 26

The eureka programme: asking what if?

Any time you are looking for a new idea, or have got
stuck implementing one you believe in, generate lots of
'what if' possibilities. Really go with your imaginings,
refuse to censor them with any common sense, enjoy
the fantasy, then review what you have dreamt of,
applying cool analysis. Was there anything feasible you
could use?

The Essence of the Thing

When we look at a Picasso painting of a dove – and he painted
several – we see the absolute minimum number of brush stokes,
lines and shapes necessary to convey what the painting means.
One of his paintings has just seven lines to create – quite
unmistakably – a dove. Picasso described his art as one of
stripping away. When Michaelangelo was asked how he went
about sculpting an elephant, he replied that he took away
everything that didn't seem to suggest the shape of an elephant.
Creative intelligence gets to the essence of things. How do we
find this?

We get to the essence of things, through pattern-detection.
We play around with forms and structures, linking our subject
matter to different contexts. Familiarity is key here: when
we really know what we are involved with, we can view it
from all sorts of perspectives, and understand structures and
meanings that others have imposed on it. It becomes easy to
prioritise through asking 'what is this really about?' When
Sally does this with her novel, she realises that, in essence,
it is about a woman librarian, defined by others as a cold
spinster, discovering her sensuality, and that it has a mid-life
self-discovery theme. When Bill tries to describe what his
service is offering people, he comes up with one word, which

determines his marketing and strategy and the essence of his business: 'fun'.

STAGE 27

The eureka programme: knowing the essence

While the project you want to make happen could be an immensely complex one, you have to be able to reduce it to its essence for it to have sense and relevance to other people, and to be able to sell it, as we shall see in the next chapter. What is at the heart of your idea? Can you express this very clearly and succinctly? As your idea progresses, you will find it helpful to check periodically how the bare bones subject matter, concerns, values and beliefs that surround your idea are fitting in with its development. Drawing spider diagrams again, or mind maps, can establish whether progress is keeping the idea true to its essence – or indeed whether, because of the opportunities presented, that essence needs to change.

For instance, unexpectedly Bill finds that some of his clients are not interested in having wine parties just for fun; they are interested in heavy-duty education about the subject. He quickly realises that he is going to have to serve two distinctively different client groups, and to offer them significantly different experiences, so will need to publicise accordingly. He also spots a potential opportunity for expansion in expert-guided tours of specific wine regions for the wine anoraks!

This chapter, combined with Chapter Three about your unconscious, gives you every tool you need to think with a huge amount of creative intelligence, to get brilliant ideas and to start to make them happen. I can't emphasise enough, though, that these are ongoing tools for life: just using them once every six months won't make new connections in your brain and won't put you into the mindset of creative intelligence. To realise your creative potential fully, these techniques need to be played around with regularly. They can spice up many a dull meeting or boring journey when your mind goes flabby.

And while at the end of this chapter, we are at a stage where creative brilliance can now be yours, at the moment it is *just* yours, alone. In this form, it won't go anywhere. Other people *have* to be involved in order for creativity to have value in the market place. So we will now move on to an activity that stalls many people in their endeavours: how to sell your creative intelligence.

7

Selling Stories

Believing — Immersing — Idea generating — Creating a Vision — Reality checking — Piloting — Realising

---

This chapter is about piloting.

I don't really want to discuss my creative process too much – what's the point really? I want people to have a visceral and emotional reaction to things. – Madonna

Talking about products was never a chore – passion persuades and by God I was passionate about what I was selling. – Anita Roddick

If you have the intimate knowledge of a product that comes with dreaming it and then designing it, I have been trying to say, then you will be better able to sell it, and then, reciprocally, to go back to it and improve it. From there you are in the best possible position to convince others of its greatness and to inspire others to give their very best efforts to developing it, and to remain true to it and to see it though all the way to its optimum point. To total fruition, if you like. – James Dyson

I am sure our urge to exchange things with one another is as innate to human nature as our urge to create. Exchanging things with one another is a way of communicating, of relationship-building and of gaining something that we would like. Exchanging is also trade and selling. The innate nature of creating and exchanging could explain why, to date, capitalism seems to be the best system we have for running our world, not that I am in favour of totally unfettered capitalism, considering the views of modern psychologists, who tend to fixate on the darker aspects of human nature.

All creators have to sell their ideas in one form or another, even if it is just to a small group of super-salespeople. And many great ideas never get realised because their originators lacked the selling skills to get the thing off the ground. This is where the piloting element comes in. Because, when we sell something, what we are doing, in essence, is taking the idea to people and saying 'what do you think of this?' You are establishing relationships with them and finding out whether the idea is relevant and coherent for them, in the same way that it is for you. One way of looking at building a business is that you are attempting to have a dialogue with as many people who are like you as possible. And in a creatively intelligent world, that dialogue will include the notion contained in this chapter, that we relate to one another via our imaginations and our emotions, as well as our reasoning.

In the cyclical process of making your ideas happen, you will need to sell and pilot repeatedly. You may have to sell your idea initially, to others who may help you implement it, then to others who will back the idea, perhaps financially, or champion it within an organisation. You will also want to sell it directly to customers or clients, for when you offer people prototypes, that is the best way to get direct and extremely useful feedback.

Piloting

Piloting is just simply making something concrete that represents your idea. If your idea is a product, then you could call it prototyping. When we pilot, we act and make something. So if you are in any way inclined to procrastination, it is important to get on with this. It could be a sampler in some form of what you want to finally produce: for Bill, it could be a talk about wine-tasting, for Sally, a blurb describing her novel and sample chapters. Piloting and getting repeated feedback on your idea is the only way to really improve it. James Dyson made over 5,000 prototype versions of cyclone vacuum cleaners over a period of three years, before coming up with his revolutionary dual cyclone cleaner.

When you pilot your idea, you have something to show people and something for them to get involved with. You'll stimulate far more feedback than if you just talk about it.

Seeing Yourself Selling

Like Sally, the wannabe novelist, you may see yourself as someone who doesn't sell in any way, shape or form. She has always been a rather thoughtful, reflective type of person and takes the view that to sell something requires a pushy extroversion that she lacks. If she's honest, she'd say that really she finds the whole idea of selling something to someone else rather intrusive. Having written her book, her idea is that an agent or publisher will take it up and will then deal with all the nasty commercial end of things like selling it.

But Sally is being rather biased and compartmentalised in her thinking here. Like a lot of people, she is assuming that 'selling' means forcing things on people that they don't want. She denies her novel has any value or interest to others in assuming this, which is not really what she believes at all, having spent a year writing it. So Sally can benefit from viewing the activity of selling rather differently.

When we sell something to others, we offer it to them. We are, in effect, saying, 'I have something here that you might like or want, and I am trying to gauge your level of interest.' Good selling will involve moving away when there is no interest, but maintaining a good relationship with a potential customer; bad selling will involve persisting in trying to sell even when it is clearly detrimental to your relationship with a customer. The latter is the result of short-term thinking and profit-driven thinking and never builds really good business relations. You end up having to devote far too much energy to finding new customers all the time, because of the trail of bad relationships you leave behind you.

Now Sally may be seeing herself as a person who couldn't possibly have anything to offer others – what many pop psychologists would call 'suffering from low self-esteem' – in which case, she is identifying herself too strongly with her novel. Of course her novel may be intensely personal, but, once created, it is something outside her that has an existence of its own. If she has the dreaded 'low self-esteem', then this is something that lurks inside her. As we know from the Virginia Woolfs and Sylvia Plaths of this world, who both committed suicide, people can regard themselves as totaly inadequate in some contexts, yet still create masterpieces. So Sally can benefit from being clear in her mind that it is not herself she is offering to others – it is her novel.

What Sally may have forgotten too, is that her novel is a piece of research, and that selling it to others is part of that ongoing research. Feedback from others will give her information about how she can improve her product, for, much as she may not like that word, that is what it is. But of course there is a difference between selling something to others that clearly solves a problem – like Viagra or slug-killer – and selling something that people may not realise that they want or need, like a novel. Sally's job is to create and stimulate interest and desire.

She writes a few tentative letters and make some phone calls to agents and publishers. She is surprised at the brusqueness and lack of interest. Discussing this with a friend, she realises that, whenever she communicates with anyone about her book, she is involved on some level with selling it. She has to drop the fantasy that people are waiting there to discover her great work and will then work out themselves how to champion it on her behalf. No, she has to roll up her sleeves, view her novel as a product and probably herself as one too, and get out there pitching. Whether she likes it or not, she has to learn to sell. Who knows, it may offer her some interesting insights into the human psyche for her fiction.

Any reservations you may hold about your ability to sell can be dealt with by replacing that word 'selling' with 'enthusing'. This is the most contagious and powerful mode of communicating, and worth mastering, whatever you do in life. It appeals to that most necessary of human emotions: hope.

STAGE 28

The eureka programme: you as a salesperson

As soon as your idea is coherent in your mind, start to talk about it and be aware that you are enthusing to others. Listen to their objections and cynical comments and work out ways of overriding these, if appropriate, with the upside of what you are suggesting. Practise enthusing about your idea to a whole range of people, so that when you come to talk about it to someone who is really significant in its implementation, you are confident and articulate about pitching. Ask people you trust for their opinions on how your pitch sounds, get training if necessary and practise with a video camera.

Pithy Pitching

Bill has done a business plan for his wine business, has approval from his bank manager and now must approach some wine suppliers and potential customers. He rather looks forward to the selling aspect. He likes talking to people, and has done well at this sort of influencing in the past. Where he may be weaker is the tactical side of promoting his business.

He has several wine suppliers to contact. The first one asks Bill to describe the business and then seems irritated by his rather meandering description. He asks Bill to call back when he has a clearer focus, even though during the phone call Bill described long-term financial projections that he felt should have been of interest. A day or two later, Bill bumps into his neighbour, also a wine buff. 'How's your enterprise coming along, Bill?' asks the neighbour. As Bill is talking, he realises that he has not encapsulated what he is doing in any kind of marketing pitch. He cannot stand at one end of a zebra crossing screaming the idea to a person at the other end, and be certain they know what he is talking about. His neighbour seems keen to hold one of his wine-tasting parties: but how would he describe it to potential guests? While Bill has done all the sensible spade-work needed to start a business properly, along with research and financial projections, he hasn't done the rather more upfront work and description of his enterprise. He hasn't thought about the creative side of selling it.

So Bill's first task is to name the business. He has to come up with something that suggests wine-tasting parties, linking the ideas of wine tasting with home delivery, via a sociable event. He comes up with various ideas: Wine Express, the Winery, the Wine Experience. None of these quite capture the spirit of the business, he feels. They don't sound like fun. He toys with something French, Bon Santé or Bon Goût. Then he realises it can be much simpler and more direct than that: why not call it The Good Taste Wine Company? This will describe, he hopes the experience that people will have when they come to the parties, but also will imply that people have 'good taste' in the aesthetic sense, in choosing to hold and attend a wine-tasting event.

Bill's choice of name fits with guidelines we give people on workshops. When you are selling ideas, it is really helpful to think about function and form, feelings and fantasies. What shape does the idea take and what is its purpose? This should be readily encapsulated in as few words as possible. Often on our workshops, we hear people go into elaborate descriptions of their ideas, which are quite engaging, but at the end of the pitch, nobody present is able to describe what the idea is and how it works. This is the pragmatic aspect of selling. People need to know very simple things like what it is and what it does. They need to know about usefulness.

Also on workshops, we hear pitches that are full of usefulness and rationale, but leave the audience emotionally and imaginatively cold. This is about consideration: how will the people you are pitching to feel about what you are selling, and how will it spark their imaginations? Bill needs an uplifting name for his business, because he wants people to feel that the parties will be fun. In using 'Good Taste', he is appealing to the imaginary qualities of aspiration: the people he is targeting will want to imagine that they are stylish and discriminating. You may hate this idea, but it works when targeted appropriately. Bill's customers will have the sense from his business that they will be getting, literally and socially, 'Good Taste'.

Bill needs to think in two different ways about his initial sales pitches. When talking to wine suppliers, they need to feel excited about the long-term potential for growth in Bill's business. He needs to feel that they are people he can trust and rely on to supply him, as and when he wants, and that the relationship can become strong enough for them to offer advice when he needs it. He needs to find a supplier who is receptive to new ideas and who won't sneer at his modest initial profit. I think you can hear here, that Bill's sales pitches to the suppliers are, yet again, research for him; will this work in terms of mutual understanding and similar goals?

With potential hosts and hostesses, he needs a slightly different approach. People will need to feel reassured that their parties will go well, that people will enjoy them and that, although Bill's business is new, he will be professional and organised. If Bill reads this book, he will almost certainly pilot a couple of parties, with groups of people who are representatively useful for feedback. Party hosts will need to be sold the idea on the basis that Bill's parties are great fun and very professional. As soon as Bill has run his pilot parties, he will have good examples of what happens and stories to use to make his pitch sound vivid and accessible.

Bill's best approach will be to research the people he is pitching to, and then to imagine what questions those particular people are likely to ask him. He should consider: In what way is my idea useful to them? What is likely to appeal to how they feel and fantasise about things? You will only be guessing some of these answers, but at least you will have thought about their IQ, and emotional and creative intelligences.

STAGE 29

The eureka programme: targeting

1. Whether your idea is a service or a product, you should be able to name it succinctly. In business, the best names often describe what the service or product gives people on the receiving end. Think of Benefit cosmetics or Kleeneze, for instance. The key questions to ask are:

> What does my idea do?
> How does my idea work?
> How does it make people feel?
> What fantasies does it appeal to?
>
> When you've answered this, you have dealt with my four Fs: function, form, feelings and fantasies. This should make you feel fabulous, darlings.
>
> 2. Describe your idea to as many people as you know, who could be targets for it. Ask them what they think of it. Then ask them if you can involve them in your pilot or prototype activity. Get more feedback. Keep asking them for suggestions. Use this dialogue to find out more about their likes and dislikes and what they really want.
>
> 3. If you've been immersed in your subject area for some time, then you should know others who share your interest. Ask them for leads if your target market is proving difficult to reach. Use the internet, and approach people for advice. Most people are flattered by this request, especially if it is phrased in a way that suggests they are, incomparably, the world's greatest expert on the subject! Offer to buy lunch for anyone who can help you.

What are your Stories and Metaphors?

In Chapter Three, I described how stories and metaphors contribute greatly to how we make sense of the world. People on the receiving end of your ideas will be looking for stories and metaphors. To sell their ideas, both Sally and Bill will need to have their background stories ready: Sally's will be about her own experiences of working in a university library, combined with the real-life adventures of a friend of hers, and

Bill's will be about always wanting to do something that involved his life's passion: wine.

Sally decides to throw herself into this selling business by researching it as thoroughly as possible. She realises that she is missing significant opportunities if she presents her novel inadequately when she does get some encouragement from an agent or publisher. She goes to a library, buys a couple of books on being a professional writer and buys lunch for a friend who works in publishing. The friend tells Sally several unexpected things: that Sally needs a dynamic one-page letter to sum up the novel and what it is about, before anyone will venture a read of it; that she needs to look at herself entirely as a product and how this product will relate to the market for the book; and that she needs to ensure that she is as media-friendly as possible.

Now Sally's novel is about a mid-life crisis, but it is a mid-life crisis with a difference in that the middle-aged woman who is the main character embarks upon an orgy of sex, sensuality and pleasure while continuing her job as head librarian at a top university. It is no coincidence, either, that Sally herself works as a librarian at a university. Sally realises that she will have to use metaphor to explain what the book is similar to, and find some metaphors that will be easily recognisable by book agents and publishers. The atmosphere of the book, she decides, is Anita Brookner gone rampant. There is something of a female Philip Larkin about the main character. The plot is not dissimilar in some ways to Shirley Valentine, and the going rampant in middle-age owes something to the The Sexual Life of Catherine M, the controversial description of a French intellectual's sexual adventures, although Sally's book is not quite so excessive.

Having got these points of reference ready for her description of her book, Sally now wants to use metaphors in her description. You may remember from Chapter Three that metaphors are links in our memories; they are a primary way of engaging other people's attention and imagination.

Metaphors are often based on the human body, movement and personal qualities, in which case Sally's novel is most definitely 'a romp'. They are often linked to games, war, vehicles and containers – in which case, her book is a war on the idea that middle-aged women are 'past it'. They can be based on places, food, drink – in which case Sally's novel is one to be enjoyed in France or Italy, on the summer break, with a glass of Sauvignon Blanc or Pinot Grigio and some succulent olives on the side . . .

Sally realises how powerful metaphors can be in conveying meaning; the three I've just described sum up the type of book it is, and the market, very quickly for others. The most effect-ive metaphors, as we might expect, are ones that many of us are familiar with in everyday life. How people see things, the weather, money, clothing, family life, religion, sports and play are all potential sources of metaphor.

Now I'm aware that you may be thinking at this point: 'yes, well, this is all well and good, but it is hardly creative, is it; there's nothing new about any of it'. Well, Sally believes her particular combination of influences to be new. Also, it is important, for the selling of her idea, that it is easily refer-enced by others. Agents and publishers will have maps inside their heads of the domains in which they operate, and Sally has helpfully created clear grid markings for them of where to place her book.

STAGE 30

The eureka programme: referencing your idea for others

1. What's the story behind your idea? Is it succinct, with some conflict or difficulties to overcome and elements of reversal? Does the conclusion form your idea? Your story shouldn't be too detailed; it is merely providing scene-setting and credibility for

your idea. It tells people where you are coming from. Your story will be useful when you are seeking press interest, too.

2. What metaphors can you use to help explain your idea? What images does it evoke and how can you use these in your description? Remember that metaphor and memory are inextricably linked. What are people going to be reminded of? Powerful ideas often take people off into slightly different worlds – the quirky realm of a university library or the sophisticated domaine of wine connoisseurship, for instance.

Apart from selling her idea, though, Sally is stumped, especially when it comes to selling herself. The only occasion she feels she has had to do this in the past is when she has gone for job interviews. Her friend suggests that she uses an idea of archetypal characters to see who she feels she would like to play.

What's Your Archetype?

Jung, who was a contemporary of Freud, with whom he fell out on some matters, popularised the idea of archetypes. He said that an archetype was an original pattern existing in the collective unconscious – that is, a collective invisible mind, or psyche. Archetypes are stories and characters that help us see ourselves in the external world; they link the conscious and unconscious mind.

I used to think that Jung's ideas were rather mystical and obscure. But his ideas get some backing from anthropological research. Donald Brown, an anthropologist, has written a book called *Human Universals*, which lists hundreds of shared traits between people, regardless of their culture. These include such gems as lying, psychological self-defence mechanisms, mothers raising their pitch when they talk to children, and a fear of snakes. Good stories and characters have a universality as well. There are about 48 different versions in the world of 'Little Red Riding Hood', where an innocent seeker is taken in by a big bad predatory wolf. Many of our archetypal ideas come from myths – ancient and modern. They will be hanging around in our unconscious memory neurons.

When we look at our own culture, we see many archetypal figures. *Sex and the City* is based on four archetypal women: the predatory one, the upper class one, the professional one and the incredibly stylish one. Bill Clinton is an archetypal homeboy made good, Tony Blair is a do-gooding public schoolboy in the tradition of Biggles or Algernon, with a religious streak thrown in. Margaret Thatcher, Hillary Clinton and Cherie Blair have all suffered from media depictions that show them to be versions of Medusa of 'The Gorgons' fame or Lady Macbeth.

Of course there are risks to appearing archetypal; you may be typecast by people, who refuse to see beyond these limitations. But, on the whole, people feel more comfortable with individuals whose presentation adds up to some sort of coherent whole. We like to deal with those who fit readily and neatly on our sense-making maps.

In the UK, William Hague, who led the Conservative Party for a while, had problems with this. He looked like a rather jolly baby, but sounded like a 55-year-old Yorkshire businessman. His self-presentation confused people and they sensed incongruity, which detracted from his considerable articulacy on the floor of the House of Commons.

Sally Finds A Character

Her friend sits down with Sally and they talk about possibilities for Sally's 'image'. They ask themselves 'what do people think about librarians?' and they come up with words like 'prim, repressed, orderly and organised, quiet, thoughtful, and wholesome'. They ask themselves what famous characters spring to mind and come up with 'Miss Jean Brodie', 'Cinderella' and Julie Andrews. They agree that Sally needs to reflect the main theme of the book, which is that appearances can be deceptive. Her friend likes the image of a French governess in a porn movie, terribly restrained, correct and with good taste on the surface, but underneath seething with passion. They decide that Sally needs to look like a rather glamorous librarian, one who is wearing a twinset and pearls, but with a suggestion of black stocking and suspender belt underneath. Sally is not slim, and her curves suit a suggestion of the 1950's, which fits this image well. She will get herself a pair of stylish cat-woman shaped glasses, some restrained reddish lipstick, a bouffant hair-do and pearl earrings, et voilá, the discreet but sensual lady authoress is born!

It may well have crossed your mind that Sally is spending a lot of time and thought on how she sells her novel and herself. She will write her letter, making it as dynamic as possible and asking for feedback; she will get photos taken; she will research agents and publishers who handle authors similar to herself. She will need to be dogged and persistent. But she will be in a much better position than someone who has done none of the above. She has bothered to think about how the book and she could be marketed to the public; and also factored in that we communicate with one another through both conscious and unconscious means. Because we are less aware of the un-conscious means, they may be doubly powerful.

STAGE 31

The eureka programme: you as archetype

1. When people meet you, can you guess who they are reminded of? Does how you look, sound and dress

match up to a coherent, congruent whole? However much you do not like the idea, when you are selling anything to anyone, you have to be aware of how your image supports the idea. Here are some very common and familiar archetypes: heroine/hero; successful businesswoman/man; caring professional-doctor; psychologist; bluestocking/nutty professor; trail-blazer; funster/jester/clown; wild woman/man; sex goddess/god; domestic goddess/god; country-dweller; city slicker/ analyst; counsellor; advocate; visionary; earth-mother; warrior. Remember all the choices you make about your presentation and send out indicators to others about where you fit on their map of archetypes. Unless you are looking for someone to take a controlling interest in your project, 'togetherness' is usually wise.

2. If your presentation needs attention, get expert advice from books, magazines and recommended image experts.

Talking and Listening

Bill feels quite confident about his self-presentation and he's learnt that he needs to be able to talk about it succinctly. He has a good name for his enterprise: The Good Taste Wine Company, which will allow him to expand into selling cheese, and pâtés, if appropriate, later on. He is wisely seeing his customers in two camps: those who will supply him with goods and those who will buy the wine via the wine-tasting parties.

But his first outing to see a wine supplier is not wholly successful. Although Bill conveys enthusiasm and has thought about what questions the supplier might ask him, he feels that he comes across as overpowering. He is so enthusiastic about his research, and all the people he has been talking to about the business, that he talks in one great outpouring. When he sits down to reflect after the meeting, he realises he has got very little information from the supplier. Once again, he just talked at him a bit too much. Once again, too, he needs to review his tactics.

Bill revisits the idea of himself as a researcher. Looking at all he has researched so far, he realises that he can prepare for future meetings by asking himself 'what particular parts of my research would be interesting to this person?' He takes an overview of his activity, and realizes that he is perhaps spreading himself too thin now. Rather than talking to his entire street about his idea, perhaps he would be wiser just targeting the three or four neighbours who are interested in wine, and who love to socialise. Perhaps it is time for him to be less lateral in his focus, and more vertical. He knows he needs to do more in-depth listening generally.

Fortunately, the wine supplier is enthused enough to suggest another meeting. This time Bill says very little. He asks instead what the supplier would like to get out of the relationship, what would her best hopes be for it, and how would she see it working. Frequently he asks her: 'What do you think about that?' He is open about his own worries about the new business, summarises quite a lot of what she says, and she, in turn, is very open back. Reservations and worries aside, the meeting is a very productive one, and Bill feels that the other wine suppliers will have to really dazzle to be better potential partners than this one.

The Meaning of Your Enterprise

Bill clarifies in his mind what benefits the business can bring his different customers. For the wine suppliers, profit, clearly, but also a sense of being involved with something new and exciting, with great potential for expansion in different ways.

Bill is very keen to be advised on the right type of wines for the tastings and after-sales. For his customers, it will be rather different. There will be novelty involved, of course, and for busy people, it is a very convenient way of socialising at home without much preparation. Bill will supply glasses, all drinks and nibbles, if wanted. The hosts receive a gift of specially chosen wine. They have a strong sense of being in a certain social group – or snobbery, if you like – and of being in a sufficiently privileged position to care about the finer things in life like wine.

And what about threats? Well, for the suppliers, the whole thing could go wrong and they might waste time and risk losing some money. For the party hostesses and hosts, the event could be a failure if Bill doesn't lead the tastings, or if people become inhibited about sampling and buying at the end of the evening. It requires quite a lot of trust to let someone you don't know very well hold a party in your house. Communication between Bill and the hosts will have to be very good beforehand.

Bill hits upon a way of both piloting his idea and getting further research. He will take some sample wine and some questions to his four bon viveur neighbours and ask them if they would mind chatting to him for an hour. What he is doing, in effect, is in-depth interviews, albeit wine-fuelled, and finding out as much as he can, about the unconscious expectations of potential customers. He notes down the same ideas that occur in all three interviews: that the events should make everyone 'feel really good'; 'feel as though they are learning in an especially jolly atmosphere' and 'make the guests feel like holding a wine party themselves'.

This relates to a very important aspect of research for selling ideas: that what people say explicitly may not reflect how they behave. We often say we believe in things because of social pressure to conform. However, when you talk to people in depth, just asking open questions, particularly asking them to describe future scenarios in some detail, you are far more likely to get at some of their very powerful unconscious beliefs and values. Not a lot of market researchers know this, as Gerald Zaltman points out in *How Customers Think*. Because people generally have such a lot in common: a small number of in-depth longish interviews can yield far more interesting research than a large sample interviewed in traditional IQ style, with tick-the-box questionnaires.

As a point of interest, Zaltman's research has shown that what people want from companies that match consumer's best interests is the feeling of it being a helpful resource, which nurtures and supports them. So we are thinking of business as researcher and helper, expert, caring parent, counsellor and builder.

Bill finds his in-depth chats and listening very useful in designing and refining his marketing materials, and in determining what his potential customers want from his business.

STAGE 32

The eureka programme: hard thinking about soft selling

1. Good selling is about research and sharing. Even the most direct selling needs to establish from the outset, via listening, whether the person on the receiving end is interested or not. Pushy selling is stupidly short-term – your customers don't come back and you constantly have to work to widen your market. If your selling is considerate and relationship-based, then it is much easier to establish a market, and sell to them again. It helps to be precise in analysing what aspects of your research will be relevant to different people. In the background is your idea and how it will work, but what is interesting, specifically,

to the person you are talking to? Bank managers and customers may well perceive different benefits and threats.

2. You are sharing your research and experience. Bill gives people a very literal taster of what his idea offers when he goes to see them as research, and takes some of his wine. It's worth being as ingenious as you can about ways of conveying and sharing an experience of your idea. Sally presents herself as an echo of her book's main character, for instance.

3. More than any other activity, good selling is about listening. Find out early on whether the person is interested in your enthusiasm and how you can match what they are interested in. Brilliant sales-people are often unobtrusive, trustworthy and use their expertise. Many years ago, I was lucky enough to have one of the UK's top car salesmen on a programme. His secret? He gave potential customers one instruction on arrival at the salesroom was: 'Hello there, I'm just over here if you need me and you'd like me to help you in any way!' His manner was so totally open, accommodating and helpful that it just seemed to make people want to buy from him.

The approach in this chapter is an unusual one to selling. It is based on the notion that we all have a powerful unconscious understanding, as described in Chapter Three. Rather than just baldly describing some benefits and generalising to everyone, it suggests going under the surface and thinking about stories, metaphors, feelings and fantasies that help communicate your idea. It uses the core ideas of creative intelligence to get backers, customers and clients engaged with your endeavour. As your idea grows bigger, though, and, inevitably if you are pursuing your idea in an organisation, you will need to involve teams of people. We are moving the principles of creative intelligence into the wider context now. Let's go there next, then.

You may be reading this chapter as someone to whom team working is very familiar, who works in a large progressive organisation where project based team-working is the norm. Even so, you may not have thought, in-depth, about what helps and hinders team creativity. So in this chapter, I want to start by looking at your attitudes towards teams, for some creative spirits dread them with a passion. Then I want to look at how to build and run 'hot' – that is, creatively intelligent – teams. As this book is based on ideas that emotions and fantasies affect people greatly, we shall investigate how these affect creative productivity. Finally, I want to look at how big units – that is, organisations – regard creative intelligence.

You as a Team Player

Until this point in the book, we have concerned ourselves with the creative intelligence of the individual. Undoubtedly it is you, the individual, who gets great ideas. But to make these ideas happen, and for these ideas to have any relevance whatsoever, we need teams. Other people need to understand your ideas, be inspired by them, build on them and put them into material form. An idea is much more likely to succeed when there is a team whose interests are vested in realising it, rather than a single individual. Even with the greatest idea in the world, you cannot be an island.

Psychologically, this is an area of rich pickings, because it is about you, the individual and your relationship with groups. The first group that most of us join is the family. So often when people have 'issues' with teams, they are often reminded of problems they have had with their families. Those unconscious and conscious memory neurons are having a chat and making connections. The team setting may remind them unexpectedly of emotions they felt in their families; team members may remind them of people they have had 'issues' with in the past. We will examine these reactions in the 'Group Mind' section of this chapter.

Here's Annie, a marketing executive:

I've always been very outspoken in groups and not afraid to air my views. In fact, I'll admit it's stronger than that – I almost experience a compulsion to be provocative and difficult. Part of this is to do with not wanting to accept assumptions and the status quo, but I've realised that it is also to do with my upbringing. My family were all combative and noisy and if you didn't hold your own, you got quashed. I think I found this harder work than everyone else in the family, because I was quieter and more reflective by inclination. But I still get a slight sense, every time I am in a meeting of 'oh my goodness I must speak up, because if I don't I won't survive here'. I've taken to reminding myself 'you're not back with the family now, you know'!

Before we look at how to form hot – or creatively productive – teams, let's reflect on your individual reactions to team-working.

STAGE 33

The eureka programme: you in a team

1. Has team membership played a big part in your history so far, or have you spent much more time doing your own thing? Have you repeatedly initiated teams or been asked to join them? Do you repeatedly play the same sort of role in teams and does this echo your family experiences in any way?

eureka!

2. Identify a positive team experience; it may not be work-related, but a charity or leisure project, for instance. What are the strengths that you brought to that experience?

3. Who needs to be in your team to help you realise your idea? Are you able to establish and articulate a vision and goals for your team?

8

Hot Teams

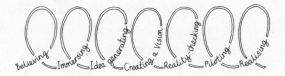

Believing — Immersing — Idea generating — Creating a Vision — Reality checking — Piloting — Realising

This chapter focuses on idea-generating, piloting and realizing.

Other people make our ideas happen and this chapter concerns itself with these relationships. On the journey from origination to realisation, our ideas will be modified and at different stages all along throughout the process will have other ideas added to them. Even if your idea seems on the surface to be a solitary one – like writing a novel, for instance – in order to make the idea happen, other people will need to contribute. Your ideas will be modified and have many other ideas added to them. You will, perhaps, start with an agent, who may introduce your work to a commissioning editor and then you will meet an editor. If the publisher is working cohesively, then you may meet cover design, marketing and selling experts, and, if you are lucky, you will get to present to the sales reps who will sell your books in the bookshops. These meetings will be crucial to the success of your book, and to creating common understanding about what it is about and where it goes in the market place.

Starting your own business, you will need to interact with others to make anything happen. You will need people to help you in your research, and people to help you with skills you lack and have no interest in acquiring: finance or administration, perhaps. You may need to get designers and printers working on your publicity. You may need to speak to experts to give you advice, and hire specialist staff to get the enterprise up and running. All organisations, both business and public sector, are systems and, inevitably then, making ideas happen involves others.

Starting a Hot Team

Robert I. Sutton, in *Weird Ideas That Work*, has some radical ideas on how to create innovative teams. He suggests hiring people who are slow to learn the organisational code, who bring a challenging perspective, rather than please-like-me-and-let-me-fit-in conformists. He suggests hiring people who make others feel uncomfortable, or who you dislike, because they will shake everyone up, and make them see things differently. And finally, he suggests hiring people you don't need, with unusual backgrounds, CVs and specialisations, again for the value they bring in with a different perspective. Advertising agencies like J. Walter Thompson deliberately recruit graduates with degrees in physics, biochemistry and biology, not obvious requirements for the arty world of advertising.

To spot creative potential for teams, listen when individuals talk for evidence of pattern-detecting, putting things into context, and ready ability to make associations. Is the person curious and interested in ideas, or are they more concerned with protecting an established and defensive 'front' in their behaviour? Oscar Wilde said 'only fools don't judge by appearances'; the way people look, the choices they have made about their appearances and their unguarded behaviour signals are good indicators about what is really going on in their minds. Even that consummate actor Bill Clinton could not convince us, due to shifty little eye movements, that 'he did not have sex with that woman, Lewinsky'!

While wanting recognition, status and money does not necessarily stop people from using their creative intelligence, it is intrinsic motivation that matters most. A key sign of creative intelligence is a strong desire to achieve. Ambition and competitiveness can be helpful, too. You'll ideally want self-motivators who are not risk-averse and who have the flexibility to be both passionate and objective about their work. I'm sure it will have struck some of you that passion and objectivity can be highly contradictory. We are asking for involvement and detachment, and the type of 'third place, triangular thinking' that was mentioned in Chapter Six.

In any creative team, you will want a certain number of confident individuals who are happy holding the conflicting desires of expressing their individuality against working communally in a team, people who are comfortable holding their individual positions along with that of group membership. Research from Harvard University shows that the best-functioning organisational boards involve a high degree of conflict amongst members. For optimum functioning, to feel like a team and to ensure that even the quieter members contribute, the best size of a team is between four and ten members. In the public sector, in the UK, this is frequently ignored. Cumbersome teams, dominated by those who shout loudest, find it difficult to demonstrate creative intelligence and to reach effective decisions.

Group Mind

So are there unconscious influences that work in groups? Here's a personal experience:

It was the first time we met as a group. There were fourteen of us. We were told to get ourselves into two fives and a four and that these were critical decisions, because we would be working in these groups, doing academic research together for four years. A hiatus occurred: some people made to-do lists, others chatted up people they liked the look of, others tried to organise the rest of us into establishing criteria for sorting people into groups, while others were childishly disruptive. We all felt confused and slightly scared, and our unconscious minds seemed in charge, as we used practised routines to help us deal with this uncertainty. What is remarkable is that, four years later, when the remnants of the group get together, we still individually perform the same routines when under threat. The same people make lists, the same people chat up others and the same people behave like twelve-year-old delinquents.

This experience has convinced me that the early days of a team's life are definitive and, if you are managing this, then it is good to be aware of how critical these early interactions are. It also has convinced me that there is such a thing as a 'group mind' – that is, patterns of thinking, response and behaviour that happen just between that particular group of people. These may be apparently small actions, like who sits where, with people sitting in the same places at every meeting, or they may be more partisan, like a couple of team members meeting privately to organise agenda items for a meeting to ensure that their priorities get pushed through. A group mind can be both conscious and unconscious; there may be practised routines that stop the team from seeing threats. A researcher called Janis identified the phenomenon known as 'group think', where individuals in the group act as gatekeepers, stopping important information that could upset the group's equilibrium from getting through.

A psychologist called Daniel Wegner researched what he called 'transactive memory systems' in couples. What he discovered was that a couple shared the responsibility of remembering specific details of their lives together. For instance, the female might remember where the door keys and cheque books were kept, while the male would remember their cross-city routes. She would remember family birthdays; he would remember what was stocked where in various DIY outlets. This kind of complementary thinking enables a couple to remember more as a unit, and it is probably also a feature of a group mind.

Unconsciously much of the time, individuals in teams take responsibilities for different types of tacit know-how and memory. They divide the unconscious work of the group, without anyone ever mentioning it.

What might be key features of the group mind of a creatively intelligent team? Well, a degree of optimism certainly, and the ability to identify with a common vision, but also the ability to critique that vision and identify progress. Humour and tolerance are helpful too. But the most critical aspect is probably trust. Do people feel that they can express ideas and feelings in the group without being attacked, and is it easy for them to maintain their individuality while still thriving in the group?

STAGE 34

The eureka programme: going beyond roles

1. We establish trust with one another through good communication, establishing common ground and openness. Formality and distinctive role-playing get in the way of this. So the more informally a group meets, and the more people chat to one another as individuals, rather than around a table where people are grouped together in roles as 'designers' or 'engineers' or 'the finance department', the better.

eureka!

2. People in creative teams need opportunities to talk about what they know about, so that their expertise and role is clear to everyone else in the team. An initial meeting where everyone offers their own story of their involvement in the group, quite informally, is a good way of doing this. After the meeting, there should be an opportunity for everyone to chat totally informally, to exchange more information.

Creative Communication in Teams

Very creative people are often very sensitive people. It is this very sensitivity to cues from their surrounding environment that makes them generate usually good ideas. According to Madonna's biographer, Randy Taraborrelli, even after decades of success, she takes criticism quite personally, ostracising certain critics for long periods of time. But, based on the construct idea in Chapter Six, if Madonna did not know what sensitivity was, how could she know how to do the opposite and be very tough at times? Whether you are a sensitive little flower yourself, or have to manage a team containing some sensitive little flowers, the handling of criticism will need to be addressed.

Now I've already gone into this in quite a lot of detail in Chapter Five, but there are a few more pointers to mention here, regarding criticism in teams. Just one highly critical individual, research shows, can put the kybosh on other people expressing their ideas freely. So monster critics have to be constantly asked for constructive suggestions, told to be quiet or asked to leave, or idea meetings have to be held when they have other commitments in their diary . . .

It helps to foster two beliefs in the team: one, that criticism of an idea is separate from the criticism of an individual. We are not just our ideas. And two, that individuals and the team have high levels of creative intelligence, so if an idea is dismissed out of hand, both the originator and the rest of the team believe that 'there are plenty more where that came from'.

Heartstorming, or Brainstorming

When I was running pilot workshops for this book, I brought up the subject of brainstorming. 'Stop,' said a participant. 'You can't use that word; you are being politically incorrect.'

'Who to?' I replied, bemused.

'People who have conditions where what they are experiencing feels like a brainstorm,' they replied.

'Lordy,' said I, 'what am I meant to call it, then?'

'Taking an idea shower,' said the participant, lamely. You can guess how I felt like responding.

One expert suggests that brainstorming should be called heartstorming, because what people really talk about in this process is what they believe and feel passionate about. So, in order to avoid issues of political correctness, perhaps we should do the same.

On-the-spot heartstorming is rarely effective, although widely practised. It favours those who are comfortable talking off the top of their heads and who like dominating and showing off in groups. The technique is much more effective when people are primed beforehand, asked to think about ideas, and then come prepared with them to the team meeting. Creative intelligence, after all, starts with the individual, and those individuals who like to encourage conversation between the unconscious and conscious neurons will need time to reflect, alone.

It is often helpful to establish guidelines for idea-generating and the building and critique of ideas and to put boundaries between these activities. Here's Robert Sutton again, describing a practice in the USA:

eureka!

At one research laboratory, no one can remember who started what has become a tradition of research and development groups. Whenever someone voices a creative idea, the person who speaks next must take the role of an 'angel's advocate', offering support. That way, the prospects are better for the survival of the fragile bud of an idea, insulating the innovative thought from the inevitable criticisms. The 'angel's advocate' normally does two things: helps to protect new ideas and to make people feel good when they are creative. As a result, people are more creative, and resonance is continually reinforced in the team.

Thinking Hats

Edward de Bono has written many books on techniques of creativity, in quite a technical and detailed way, but my favourite of all his techniques is called 'Six Thinking Hats'. In this, he suggests people wear differently coloured hats in teams representing different functions of communication. These are:

White hat: seeking information
Red hat: feelings and intuitions
Black hat: caution and critical judgement
Yellow hat: logically positive, seeing benefits
Green hat: championing new ideas, new ways, different explanations
Blue hat: overseeing the process of communication, chairing

Another way of doing this would be for people to take different roles in team meetings. Someone could play researcher, another builder, another cautious critic, another mind reader and another chairperson. The researcher would be seeking information and championing new ideas and different explanations, the builder would be seeing the benefits and adding ideas, the cautious critic would be using a great deal of their traditional IQ, and the mind reader would be sensing and intuiting all over the place, gathering unconscious messages, feelings and hunches. The chairperson would be keeping a detached eye on people staying in their roles, and keeping the meeting's agenda on track.

Other ways of using these techniques are to get the whole team to be researchers and builders while generating an idea, then after the idea has incubated for a while, going through phases where the whole team cautiously criticises and mindreads, then finally, collectively, everyone coolly stands back in a detached way, and analyses the whole process and who did what.

These ideas can take the threat out of quite charged situations. Asking someone to be 'a little less black hat, and a bit more yellow, please' is a light way of saying 'stop being so critical and try to be a bit more positive'. Teams need to be clear about their objectives – when they are meeting to express, build on and explore ideas lots of research and building, and when they are meeting to criticise ideas and express caution. When ideas need developing, the chairing role will become very important in getting everyone to suspend critical judgement and ask more about how the idea would work and why the person feels passionate and committed about it. The chair may have to stop other innovators in the team from coming in with their own ideas, distracting the group from sufficiently exploring the first.

No teams can be sizzling and sparky all the time; if they were, they would just combust – in a rather messy fashion. But hot teams do seem to manage to keep momentum over the long haul and to pick themselves up after a dip in activity and energy. Variety and stimulation are the keys here: holding team meetings in different environments, getting the team involved in tangential but inspiring action, and reconfiguring the group when necessary.

I want to base a final comment on my happy experiences

working for Alfresco TV. Television production is very team-focussed, quite creative and usually works to tight budgets and time deadlines. In these circumstances, teams create effectively when every member is quite secure about their own role and specialisation and respects those of other people, when the task is very clearly focussed and when, above all else, key individuals create an atmosphere of fun and enjoyment.

STAGE 35

The eureka programme: sensitivity, hats and the pub

1. If you are one of the many people who hold back from expressing your ideas in teams, because of your fear of shame and humiliation, remind yourself that *you* are likely to be your own harshest critic. Plunge in and speak up, but don't feel that this needs a personality change. Indeed you can show your sensitivity by using phrases like 'this may seem like a radical idea . . .' or 'some of you may find this whacky but . . .' Preface your idea with how you imagine it might be received. But still, still, still express it. Because if you don't, well, nobody will ever know that you had an idea.

    Humour is very useful in these circumstances, too, especially self-directed comments like: 'Before I describe my idea, you know how sensitive I am, and if you say anything nasty, you will probably make me cry'. It is easier for others to be direct if they know that we are taking our hyper-sensitivity with a pinch of salt and a pinch of humour. When you are managing a team where some people are sensitive to criticism, then encouraging a humorous atmosphere, where individual foibles are tolerated and joked about, can help dispel touchiness and over-sensitivity.

2. Getting people to play specific roles when discussing ideas, whether you use the language of researcher, builder, critic, etc., or thinking hats, is very useful. Just to remind you, this idea can be used in pairs, threes or even individually, as we examine our own ideas from these different perspectives. The first time you describe an idea to someone, you could ask them to build first, and then later to criticise and think of its shortcomings.

3. You are possibly aware that there are lots of different courses and theories around about team-building. My favourite one, and one that I know to be effective is called 'the going to the pub' programme. People drop roles, respond to one another as human beings, and usually discover what it is that makes each other tick. Budget for it!

When Hot Turns to Cold

The shelf life of a creatively intelligent team is probably, at absolute maximum, three years. Inevitably after that time, patterns of thinking and behaviour will start to repeat themselves in cycles, becoming tighter and tighter around the throat of the team, until they eventually strangle it. But teams can lose energy and momentum, too. One definition of creativity is that it is about communication between internal reality and external reality, and when teams lose energy and momentum, they have usually lost external focus. Several ways of remedying this, then, are bringing in some new blood to the team in order to strengthen its external focus, putting the team into new environments, where they have to concentrate on external reality or refocussing them some way on external reality.

Stan runs a team of product developers, and says:

eureka!

My team had a really busy run of about two years, coming up with loads of great ideas and being the centre of attention in the business. Then the organisation decided to go through a period of consolidation and we changed momentum, working on much more detailed, longer cycle research projects. I don't know what happened – it seemed like collective burnout, but we experienced a strange collective feeling of anti-climax and exhaustion. I thought I had better let it ride for a while, as a sort of recovery period, but then I started to get worried. It didn't seem like I needed to dissolve the team and start afresh, but I was running out of alternatives. Then I went to a conference and met someone with a similar role to mine at an American company. One of his remits was to build greater international ties, and I was telling him about my team, so incredibly, he invited us all over to visit his company in Detroit. It was fantastic, completely reinvigorating and shifted the team's perspective right out toward the big picture.

The study of group dynamics concerns itself with unconscious influences and exchanges that go on in groups. A lot of this study is Freudian in orientation, with a focus on dark repressed forces, rather than my preferred scanner-like version of the unconscious. Nevertheless, observations made by group dynamics experts are fascinating. They can be seen to represent common fantasies held by many of us, and as example of typical ways in which the goals of the imagination in the unconscious may clash with the goals of the conscious mind.

Team Fantasies

One of these group dynamics experts was a man called Wilfred Bion and he came up with three common fantasies that team members experience. The first was a fantasy of dependency based on the leader: that the leader would protect the group or, alternatively, that the leader might destroy the group. We can surmise the sort of behaviour that would occur in a group where this fantasy was strong: team members would be too reverential to the leader, perhaps behaving like children towards her or him – and both envious of, and rather cross with their dependency on, the leader. Where they feel the leader has let them down, they would feel mightily betrayed, but also guilty about their own betrayal of the guru.

The second fantasy Bion identified was fight or flight. It's often said that during wartime or conditions of hard economic trading, countries and businesses are at their most unified and productive. This is due to the cohesive influence of everyone seeing themselves fighting with someone else. In creatively intelligent teams, this may be fighting with the rest of the straights in the organisation, or fighting with all the other boring people in the world who don't understand what the team is about. Flight, predictably enough, involves the sense that a team is fleeing from the control and responsibility of the managerial world or some other care-worn place, and are out on their own, blazing a new trail. Flight and fight fantasies are usually invoked by fear, anger and suspicion. They often result in the team imagining they are more isolated than is really the case.

The third fantasy Bion described was a very pleasant one: Utopia. In this fantasy, a single team member or a pair of members as a kind of Messiah or Mary and Joseph – would produce something or someone to save the team. (Sounds as if quite a few religions could be based on this one.) Emotions engaged here would be hope, faith, enthusiasm and disillusionment. There may be all sorts of religious and sexual imaginings going on here also; that two of the team may literally produce a saviour, for example, or that suffering extensively in the present may be worth it in the long run.

While, in the short term, these fantasies may help a team

function, long term they can sap energy and momentum from the team and cause it to lose touch with reality. People will not work well together when they are imagining members of the team are like their parents, god-like, or constantly working at procreation! To refocus the team, concentrating on its task and external environment can help.

Here's Stan again:

A couple of years ago I had a team where there were all sorts of strange undercurrents. They were young and very keen, but some of them kept behaving like little lost children, and others were like Pollyanna – completely visionary and unrealistically optimistic, like they had swallowed some happy pills, or something. I wasn't sure how to handle this at all, and felt out of my depth, so I did something very manipulative . . . I invented a new external focus. I told them that the deadline for the project we were working on had been brought forward by two months. They just had four weeks left to complete it. I suspected that I was being too parental in my role as team leader, so after a fortnight I took two weeks, holiday. Amazingly, they completed the project on time, but, more significantly, they seemed to have grown in maturity and confidence dramatically over that period.

STAGE 36

The eureka programme: warming up cold teams

1. Where you are leading a team and being the focus of fantasies or experiencing unhelpful fantasies yourself (they can of course be merely enjoyable, the problem arises when they make you respond in a very irrational way to others), then get out of the role generated by the fantasy. If you are the subject of

the fantasy, have a frank discussion with the fantasist to point out that, a) you are not Margaret Thatcher (dependency fantasy), b) the team is not at war with the world or a sanctuary from it (flight or fight), and c) you are neither the Buddha, God, or Mary looking for Joseph (utopian fantasy). If you are the fantasist, compartmentalise your imaginings and look outside them to see what is really going on in reality. Don't feel guilty – remember, imagination is a marvellous thing, but it may be getting in the way of your functioning effectively in this instance.

2. Where practical difficulties are getting the team down, then these need to be tackled first before re-iterating the vision for the team. In this instance, it is reality-checking that needs to take precedence.
When the team feels that practical difficulties are on their way to being resolved, then the vision can be reiterated through people talking about their shared enthusiasms and passions.

   It is this common ground that will make the team tick again.

Organisations and Creative Intelligence

Creative intelligence can be a real problem for organisations. If an organisation is to survive, be resilient and grow, then it must harness the stuff. The trouble is, creatively intelligent people can be subversive, tend to question fundamental assumptions and givens, and do not usually worry too much about fitting in. Creative intelligence and compliance are two ideas that never go together. So, while organisations need creatively intelligent people, they can be difficult to manage, especially where to manage means to command and control.

Hilary Burden was a magazine editor for many years who

left organisational life, and wrote about her disillusionment in London's *Guardian* newspaper, in an article entitled 'I Quit!':

> . . . *modern boards have developed into committees of people amassing power and shareholder wealth, rather than real creativity, and who have little to do with actually creating the products they sell. In my experience, a corporate apartheid exists between those who create, nurture and polish ideas, and those who reap the material rewards . . .*
>
> *They want passion in their organisations, but when they woo it, they try to control it because they fear it more than anything. So creative energy is tamed and cooled by the twin weapons of hierarchy and silence . . . This isn't so much about employee rights. It's about the management classes getting out of their comfort zone and learning to re-engage with creativity, and it's about employees learning not to give the best of themselves away.*

As I mentioned at the beginning of the book, organisations are not very keen on the word 'creativity' either. It is all a bit open-ended, vague and arty-farty. Instead, they prefer to talk about 'innovation', meaning creativity that produces things, which can then be used and sold.

What Hot Teams Need

Sue is asked to recruit a team for a law firm, which she has recently joined as head of marketing. Her idea is that she would recruit quite gradually, over a period of several months, to pick people who would really fit together well. Unfortunately, this is not how the partners in the firm see it at all. She is to cobble together her team within a matter of weeks, because 'creative marketing that sees off the competition' has to be her top priority. And for that, she needs to get on to something of a war footing. Sue wonders whether her decision to join this particular firm was the right one . . .

Viewing creative intelligence as a means of avoiding problems imposes limitations on individuals and organisations. Of course, being innovative keeps an organisation 'ahead of the game', but when it is a reaction to something, its point of origin is always going to be the need to ward off the threat of another organisation. Therefore, the company's position will be a defensive one, which implies imposing barriers and boundaries that will close off sources of inspiration.

Organisations must seek to be innovative for their own sake, because they understand the ever-shifting unpredictability of the world in which they operate and because there is a love in the organisation of curiosity, research and experiment. They must have the constructive orientation of wanting to make a thing and to bring something into being.

Again, like individuals, organisations must prioritise learning rather than performing in order to be innovative. The disgraced Enron Corporation of the USA prided itself on recruiting 'major talent' and 'stars' rather than employees who might learn something while doing their jobs. The company's culture became about concealment of mistakes, preserving face and looking good, to the detriment of ethics and good practice. An organisation putting constant pressure on teams to succeed, will be detrimental to innovation. Shakespeare, Darwin, Picasso and Madonna all succeeded through producing a wider range and more ideas than their contemporaries: teams must follow the same course of action. In many organisations, failure is seen as taboo: people learn to pass the buck, pretend it never happened and attribute it to external factors. If organisations want innovative teams, they must encourage a climate where people can say, 'Hands up, yes, that was me who messed up, but you know I have learnt a heck of a lot from it!' This climate must come from the very top of the organisation and should permeate organisational language; the more that projects are seen as experimental pieces of research and reviewed as such afterwards, the better. And people in the organisation are best viewed as researchers and builders, rather than skivers or worker drones.

Linked to this also is the value the organisation puts on the critical thinking of traditional IQ compared to the value of experiential learning. Where he who sneers loudest is promoted and seen to be valued most, over she who says, licking her wounds, 'Well I learnt a lot,' then innovation is likely to be stifled. People won't express their ideas because they don't want to look silly and be sneered at. If people are likely to be ridiculed and humiliated for making mistakes, then they will be reluctant to experiment. They will play safe, avoid risks and keep a low profile. Creatively intelligent organisations view mistakes as good learning curves.

But what about profit and cost, I hear you scream? Aren't unsuccessful experiments costly and time-consuming? Well, as Robert Sutton points out in *Weird Ideas*, the biggest disincentive to innovation in teams is constantly reminding people of the need to make money. Financial and recognition factors are about external motivation, not the type of motivation that keeps people going over the long haul. Of course, profit and cost need to be factored in, but from a distance. A discreet eye needs to be kept on it, one that understands how central and critical innovation is to the organisation. Financial managers are best ring-fenced and kept away from the innovators, inquiring and investigating only when absolutely necessary.

Other innovation-killers include routine, lack of diversity and repeating tradition. I've mentioned a couple of instances in this book already, where people have been told, 'You must produce X number of ideas in Y time and we need them regularly once a month'. This can only encourage in-the-rut, repetitious, well-established thinking routines. So, where job-cycle and project times need to vary, it is better to ask a group to come up with several ideas over a long period of time, rather than demanding regular idea instalments. Bearing in mind that routine and rules usually need to exist for safety reasons, the greater the routine, the more anaesthetised to risk people will become. It may well be worth asking 'what useful purpose does this routine serve?' and where the answer is 'none', scrapping it.

Here's Professor Henry Mintzberg again:

We've become prisoners of measurement: audits, league tables, targets. It just destroys creativity. Look, I'm not opposed to measuring things that can be measured – I'm opposed to letting those things drive everything else out. It has some destructive effect in business, but in education and healthcare, it's absolutely devastating.

What would happen if we started from the premise that we can't measure what matters and go from there? Then, instead of measurement, we'd have to use something very scary: it's called judgement. A society without judgement is a society that's lost. And that's what bureaucracy does: it drives out judgement.

Any system, biological or social, works better when it has plenty of variance. This means diversity of membership – particularly important for innovative teams. Lotus Systems in America carried out a fascinating experiment where they gave the HR department the CVs of the first 40 people to join the company. Its executives felt that the original commitment to the diversity that had inspired the company in its early days had got lost, and that they were recruiting a very limited and homogenous type of person. When the unsuspecting HR Department looked at the founders' CVs, not one of them was called for interview. Clearly, their creative sparks were no longer appropriate. The characters who originally got the whole enterprise underway would no longer have been let in past the front door.

An organisation that is too precious about honouring tradition and repeating it is unlikely to encourage the creation of innovative teams. People usually keep repeating the same formula because it makes them money, which is fine while the market or environment remains stable, but if there is a big change in what people want or how the environment works, then they can be in big trouble. At least they won't be able to say that you didn't warn them . . .

Signs of Organisational Creative Intelligence

You may want to take your idea to a big organisation or join one where you can be more creative. So here are some signs that an organisation values creative intelligence. Where a company is a big bureaucratic machine, with well-established practices, you may have to search hard for a part where creative intelligence is encouraged. Gareth Morgan, in *Images of Organisation*, essential reading for anyone interested in organisational life, offers different metaphors for organisations. One that feels like a huge machine is much less likely to foster creative intelligence, than one seeming more like a living organism. You can often tell by a visit to the place: amongst book publishers, for instance, there are some that welcome visitors very personally and make interaction between authors and employees very personal, whilst others feel like big impersonal book factories. Ideas and individuals get treated differently in these contrasting business settings.

Apart from obvious signs of diversity, like different types of people working in the company, how is variance handled in other ways? Are people encouraged to become multi-skilled so that they can move around within the organisation? Is there a lot of cross-department communication? Does the organisation regard its staff as flexible, full of potential and worthy of nurture and respect? The way people talk about the company can tell you a lot about it. Note the extent to which the organisation focuses inwardly on itself and the extent to which people talk about the environment in which it operates. An organisation with a strong outward focus is likely to be more creatively intelligent than one that is busy contemplating its own navel.

Many organisations, which should be creatively intelligent, make themselves less so via their appraisal and reward systems. Managers who control routine work and police efficiency receive the best rewards, and creative people are judged by the same criteria. Unfortunately they can never live up to these demands; they are too busy having ideas and making things to concern themselves with cost-cutting, controlling things and making themselves look good.

Creatively intelligent organisations will have learning and change at the very centre of their identity. If there is a board, then there should be strong representation on it from people with interest in these areas. Training and development should be taken very seriously, and not be a bolt-on activity for 'Tracey in accounts, who plans the annual conference'. Job specifications will be about the purpose of the job and what teams need to achieve, not about how they need to do their work. Look for symbolic evidence: if the surroundings and printed material are inordinately dull, this may not be a place where a creative flower like you could blossom.

STAGE 37

Practical eureka: finding creative organisations

1. Size can make businesses less creative. Smaller, less
   hierarchical organisations must be more flexible and

responsive to market needs than great big monoliths. In small operations, it may be easier to get ideas implemented and company culture may be less risk-averse.

2. In my experience, there can be great differences between organisations in the same sector, as to how they handle feedback, decision-making and mistakes. A creatively intelligent organisation is likely to encourage very open feedback, with systems in place to criticise those at the very top of the hierarchy. Where posturing and preserving face are more important, there will be less encouragement to innovate and risk failure. So find out about a company's feedback systems. Hewlett-Packard used to encourage every employee to have a prototype on their desk, to think about and criticise.

3. Typical signs of creative organisations are employee suggestion boxes and envelopes that go directly to the top, informal clothes (formality creating distance) and cross-departmental involvement. At the Dyson factory, every new employee assembles a cleaner in its entirety on the first day. Creative organisations tend to encourage lots of dialogue rather than more impersonal communications via memo and e-mail. Look for these signs.

By the end of this chapter, your team should be functioning effectively to implement your or their ideas. Now we move up a notch again, to look at how we disseminate creative intelligence very widely, so that you can make your ideas happen on a large scale. We look at how to create wildfire.

Creating Wildfire

Believing — Immersing — Idea generating — Creating a Vision — Reality-checking — Piloting — Realising

This chapter is about realizing.

From small sparks of creative intelligence can come wildfire.

What is it that ensnares creative intelligence, which makes ideas viral, that makes business ideas boom, and turns designs, books, films, TV shows and computer games into bestsellers? Is it timing, people or particular influences in the surroundings at a specific time? Well, probably a combination of all three. People, their surrounding and influences at the time are interdependent. We need places that give us stimulation, times for reflection and opportunities to see things differently, all of which build creative intelligence. Places need people with a drive to create to want to live and work in them. You've probably experienced the revitalising effect of a trip somewhere new, when you return home full of new ideas. You've probably also been to places, or, if you are lucky enough, you will live in one now, where you think: 'yes, this is where I could really excel and produce wonderful results'.

eureka!

This chapter is about these aspects, people and their surroundings, and deals with two key questions: what can you do to make your ideas highly contagious and how can people design surroundings that will encourage creative intelligence to flourish? It is about realising your ideas, big-time.

People

Small ideas can tip dramatically and quickly into epidemic popularity, according to Malcolm Gladwell in his bestselling book *The Tipping Point*. Using examples like Hush Puppy shoes, the children's TV show *Sesame Street* and the success of New York City's Zero Tolerance crime policy, he describes how small ideas can spread prolifically. Not surprisingly, there is no unifying principle: Hush Puppies became popular through people – 'early adopter' trendsetters in clubs reinventing them as fashion items; Zero Tolerance worked through enforcing care and respect for surroundings by clamping down vigorously on small anti-social crimes like drunkenness and graffiti. This latter idea suggests that our surroundings may affect our behaviour more than we realise, and, therefore, that putting people into good and protected surroundings makes them behave better. But it is the people factor to which the author rightly gives most priority.

Only Connect

Certain people are 'connectors' – natural facilitators – people who love meeting new people and who take delight in working out what these new people might have in common with some of the others on their huge database of contacts. Connectors have a view of the world that centres on a key principle of creative intelligence: that life is a network of contacts and that we are linked together like spider webs. This is one of the key thinking skills described in Chapter Six.

People who are connectors love social contact and investigating different worlds. They tend to have a very wide circle of acquaintances, with whom they will be very easy going, but whom they have no desire to get to know better. Their function is to make social glue, to spin bigger webs so that more and more people can network. Not surprisingly, connectors often make very successful business people, because, as they spin their webs, more and more people get to know about what they do, and may buy into it. Connectors practise what is called the 'weak tie' – where they know lots of people but few in great depth – a pattern of relationships that is increasingly prevalent in the loose communities most of us live in today. A connector can be a frustrating individual with whom to have a deeply meaningful and intimate relationship.

Who do you know who is a connector?

Six Degrees of Separation

Professor Mark Granovetter, in his book entitled *Getting a Job: A study in contacts and careers*, was one of the first people to identify the 'weak tie'. He showed that casual acquaintances were better for finding jobs than close friends. These close friends share similar information to you, but the 'weak tie', who may be a friend of a friend, will know about opportunities beyond those known by your close circle. Presumably the same guideline applies for finding opportunities to exploit ideas, too. You gotta get people talking.

Stanley Milgram, a social psychology researcher, set up some 'weak tie' research. He sent a letter to 160 people and urged them to return this letter to a specific individual, a stockbroker. None of these people knew the stockbroker. All the letters were returned to the stockbroker; in most cases, there were five to six links made before the letter reached him. A very large percentage of the letters ended up in the hands of three individuals, who were the last links before the stockbroker. This led Milgram to describe a theory of six degrees of separation between people, and this idea was further popularised by John Guare in his play entitled *Six Degrees of Separation*, about a con man operating in the art world, claiming to be someone who had contacts, which did not really exist.

You may have seen *Six Degrees of Separation* type articles in newspapers, where a celebrity or famous politician is placed at the centre of the web, and then drawn around them are all their network of contacts and how they are linked. Further analysis of projects these celebrities or politicians have been involved in, would inevitably show how obtaining jobs via this network of contacts works.

Networking

These ideas about networking have been championed in the form of 'network science', which is 'a new science of creativity, change and forecasting' that is revered by social commentators and futorologists. Network science research has looked at the billion or so websites on the internet and how they are connected. In *Linked: How Everything is Connected to Everything Else and What it Means for Business, Science and Everyday Life* (phew, some title, eh?), Professor Albert-Laslo Barabasi describes how the web has 'very connected' nodes that shape the way the network works. We might expect a very popular search engine like Google, for instance, to be one of these very connected nodes. They are like massive motorway junctions that link up several motorways.

Being very connected today has little to do with where you are geographically. You can live next door to someone with whom you have absolutely nothing in common, but be in contact with several hundred people in the world, via e-mail and mobile telephone, who share your interests.

creating wildfire

A Swedish philosopher named Alexander Bard has predicted that democracy and capitalism are about to be replaced by a new system: netocracy. He predicts that global networks, rather than nation states, will be the world power brokers of the future. These will be controlled by 'netocrats' who tell the underclass, the 'consumtariat', where and what to buy. Bill Gates would be an example of a worthy netocrat, someone who donates large amounts of money to good causes. But there can be a darker side to all of this too. Al Qaeda were organised in a netocratic fashion. Politicians also can activate the netocracy, with Bard citing the example of the deceased Pim Fortuyn in Holland, who appeared to tip very rapidly from having no support at all in the electorate to predictions that he could expect 20% of the electorate to support him. His advantage over the others? Hundreds of web pages and a website, all waiting to be activated. The former USA Democratic contender to lead the party, Howard Dean, used the internet to build spectacular support for his campaign, both in terms of numbers of people and donations, through websites dealing with issues relevant to potential supporters.

Another group of people who contribute to wildfire are Mavens. These are anoraks, really; people who like collecting a lot of data about a particular subject, and will know lots of obscure facts about it. They are the sort of people who know the price of bananas in every store in town, where to get amazing Shiatsu massages or what is absolutely the best lipstick in the world for durability. These people are extremely curious, read widely and glean information from all sorts of unexpected sources. Whereas connectors build relationships, mavens build information links. Many of the reviews written on Amazon.com for the more obscure titles have a maven-like quality about them. Expertise rather than sociability is their game and, if you have a great idea, then you want the mavens in your field to know all about it. Are you a maven yourself or do you know any?

eureka!

Finally, the Tipping Point identifies a third group of people essential to making ideas epidemically popular, and they are salespeople. What this group is about is emotional contagion. They are readily trusted, persuasive, credible individuals whose enthusiasm for ideas and products is such that it will influence others in large numbers. Clearly, it helps idea dissemination to have some salespeople on your side – if you are not one yourself.

STAGE 38

The eureka programme: connectors, mavens and salespeople

1. Identify your own inclinations first. Can you exploit your connector, maven or salesperson tendencies? You will need to be able to sell, to some extent, to make your ideas happen, unless you are extremely fortunate and know someone who shares your involvement and passion for your idea and can do it for you. Based on the model in this book of creative intelligence, with its emphasis on immersing yourself in subject matter, my guess is that most creative people have maven tendencies, and know their subjects in great depth, which makes them capable of making unusual connections. Mavens are easily reached via web sites and specialist organisations.

2. So what about finding connectors and salespeople to help you? The first requirement is to talk about your idea to as many people as possible, both formally and informally, and to ask if they know anyone who could help. You might want to set up an audience-grabbing talk through an organisation, or a workshop on a related subject, which you market yourself. The web, obviously, is a source to use in order to contact people who network in your subject matter. Asking

leaders in your field for advice may be helpful too; the worse thing that can happen is that they turn around and say 'no'. This is a rejection to your request, not to you personally.

3. Turn yourself into more of a connector or sales-person. Hosting events of one form or another is an easy way to get into the role. You could hold a 'launching my idea' party at your home, and invite lots of chatty people who will talk about it with one another and afterwards. If you can provide them with 'goody bags' that remind them of the event in some way, so much the better. And what about your friends? They must include some connectors or salespeople, who could give you friendly advice about what to do to get people talking.

The Zeitgeist

Is there an element of luck in how ideas become popular at specific times? Probably. But the 'zeitgeist', or 'what's in the ether at a specific time', will be a significant contributory factor to whether your idea takes off or not. Beliefs about what is in the zeitgeist are powerful influences on whether people buy ideas or not. As someone said to me early on, when the idea for this book was mooted, 'Oh the unconscious is so NOW.' Whatever your idea is, you want buyers to think 'this idea is so NOW'!!!

The zeitgeist is the spirit of the time, how people are thinking and feeling generally at any one time. One of the truths that I have learnt during my research for this project is that, while creative intelligence originates with the individual, we human beings have far more in common with one another than we have differences. For anyone wanting to create wildfire from the early spark of an idea, this commonality is worth studying. And you don't have to study psychology to do this.

eureka!

To some extent, the zeitgeist is created by the media, that is through the trends they tell us are happening in society. But there are always exceptions that disprove this, and quite often the media reports on something that is already well-established rather than a trend in embryo form. The best-selling book, Schott's *Miscellany*; the fashion for exposing one's midriff (she said, in disapproving middle-aged-spread tones); the tendency towards holidaying at home in the UK rather than travelling abroad are all trends at the time of writing that have happened without much guidance from the media.

Being open to the zeitgeist is part of a creatively intelligent mindset. It is not a stage-by-stage technique you can perfect sequentially. It is about not rushing to think in established ways in order to maintain the stability of your own world view, but about keeping an open and receptive mind. It is about stopping and looking at things. George Orwell, one of the most imaginative of writers, described himself as having 'slight literary ability, but great power of facing unpleasant facts'. This is living slightly dangerously – by getting out there and seeing and experiencing – but then courage and creativity have always gone together. You put your ideas out into the zeitgeist, see how they work, refine them according to feedback and then try again. It is this 'refining according to objective feedback' that the Tipping Point describes as 'stickiness': making ideas popular, not based on intuitive feelings about what will work, but, on detailed reality-checking about what works. James Dyson describes his development of the dual cyclone cleaner as a seemingly endless tweaking and refining, to create the perfect product.

STAGE 39

The eureka programme: your zeitgeist

1. Your subject area will have its own particular zeitgeist
   to do with what people are currently concerned with,

what research areas are of interest and what the key current dilemmas are. What are common characteristics of people who share an interest in your subject area? Are you able to identify this and describe it? Knowing this will help if you want to create wildfire with your ideas.

2. You limit your exposure to the zeitgeist if you just read left-wing or right-wing newspapers, and spend time exclusively with people who share your world view. You will limit your exposure if you just spend time with people who are the same age as you or who do the same work as you do. Read *New Scientist*, *The Economist* and *Prospect* to extend your worldview. As the government keeps urging farmers: diversify, diversify, diversify!

3. Set time aside for observation. This instruction legitimises your spending time staring out of the window in Starbucks, gazing at interesting individuals on the tube (but be careful . . .), and hanging around in parks and just watching the world go by. A part of your mind is just watching, recording and noting details of interest. You are not loafing; you are absorbing the zeitgeist.

Forget Work-life Balance

When Malcolm Gladwell describes ideas that took off like wild-fire, he talks about a book entitled *Divine Secrets of the Ya-Ya Sisterhood*, written by an ex-actress named Rebecca Wells. The book was well-received to begin with, but not sensationally so, yet still it became a huge success over a period of time. One of the things that it had going for it was that it was a perfect book-club choice, with a strong storyline about the relationship between mothers and daughters, and also straddled popular and literary fiction. It fitted well into the current networked world of women readers who belong to book clubs. Connectors and mavens would have been talking about it, and Rebecca Wells herself was a gifted saleswoman, who acted out the various characters of her book in her readings with drama and impact. Soon people were turning up in their hundreds to listen to her excerpts of what had gained cult popularity. Rebecca Wells took a whole year off to do nothing other than promote her book.

While it may be unfashionable to say so, I suspect you cannot create wildfire with your ideas while having some idealistic 'work-life' balance. If you are really enjoying releasing your labours on to the mass market, it wouldn't seem to be, something you would want to compartmentalise anyway. It won't matter that you have to fiddle with a project for a couple of hours on a Saturday night, or meet some backers for Sunday brunch. A work-life balance matters most to people who don't like their work very much, I suspect.

Now I am probably going to make myself unpopular here with some of you, but I am always meeting people who say they would like to create more, but domestic life, or earning a living, or stroking the cat just seems to get in the way. If you really want to do it, you do. You don't seek balance; you seek total and utter engagement. And it is that energy and commitment that propels a small idea to create wildfire. Forget the work/life division; instead, merge them, for that is what those whose ideas create wildfire do. Their work becomes their life, and life would be unimaginably dull without it.

STAGE 40

The eureka programme: no excuses

You can stop making excuses that take you away from your creative goals by making those creative goals, and

> the vision you want to achieve, the most important thing in your mind. Sit still for five minutes and just visualise what you want to make happen, and note how you feel about it. Then ask yourself how important, comparatively, is hoovering the bedroom or tidying your desk?

Input and Output

Creative intelligence is about input being transmogrified by thinking and imagination into output, in the form of ideas. Input from the endless clothes racks of Next, or wall-to-wall reality television, or the anaesthetising effects of junk food are unlikely to result in great output. You can shop, watch and eat so that you dull your senses, veg out and become incapable of making anything. Or you can live so that you put stimulating input in – via what you read, eat, see and who you talk to – and produce better output.

Frequently we may not be aware of the extent to which the environment is influencing our responses. An experiment set up a group of men who were to walk, individually, over a hazardous bridge. Half-way along, they met an attractive woman, who asked them some research questions. At the end of her questions, she gave them her phone number and suggested they gave her a call should they wish to see her again. All the men had slightly raised stress levels because of the context.

When the experiment was repeated in safer surroundings, with the men strolling through a park, and meeting a woman who interviewed them on a park bench, what followed was interesting. Not nearly so many men who had met the woman in a safe environment called her as did those who had talked to her on the bridge. They remembered feeling aroused on the bridge, but did not discern between arousal because of the slight danger and arousal from the woman's attractiveness. Clearly, then, the environment where we sell our ideas may matter greatly to the response they encourage in others.

In *The Rise of the Creative Class*, Richard Florida has described his research into what makes creative intelligence thrive in certain places:

> *I have come up with a handy metric to distinguish those cities that are part of the Creative Age from those that are not. If city leaders tell me to wear whatever I want, take me to a casually contemporary café or restaurant for dinner, and, most importantly, encourage me to talk openly about the role of diversity and gays, I am confident their city will be able to attract the Creative Class and prosper in this emerging era. If, on the other hand, they ask me to 'please wear a business suit and a tie', take me to a private club for dinner, and ask me to 'play down the stuff about bohemians and gays', I can be reasonably sure they will have a hard time making it.*

He champions the New Growth Theory of economics, which says that a good idea, like the wheel, can be used over and over again, with increasing returns. It can also be built upon with corresponding bigger returns – hence the double-decker bus, presumably. He talks about human creativity being the ultimate intellectual property, in that it generates patents, copyrights and trademarks. Increasingly, he believes our economy will be based on this creative captial, which will concentrate itself in particular places rather than in organisations. Places need to have a people or creativity climate more than a business one. It is people who generate social and economic change, rather than technology, he believes.

Richard Florida's research indicates that cities are better off encouraging diversity, different lifestyle options and amenities that support these, rather than subsidising companies, stadiums and retail centres, if they want to thrive as creative centres. A major research university helps a city attract the creatively intelligent. Immigrants, bohemians, gays and young people all help with these aims too. Manchester tops the list as the UK's top creative hot-spot. What Florida calls 'leveraging authentic cultural assets' is important too, and he cites Dublin as an example of a creative centre that has used existing historical buildings and traditional Irish culture to do this.

STAGE 41

The eureka programme: using the environment

1. If you can choose a conducive environment in which to sell your ideas, so much the better. Try to choose a setting where there are lots of potential customers around for your specific idea. If Bill, with his wine business, can persuade a backer to go for a drink with him in an upmarket, busy wine bar, so much the better. The backer will be surrounded by Bill's potential customers. And if Sally, with her 'mid-life' novel, can suggest a meeting with an agent in a museum or art gallery café, then so much the better, as she will be surrounded by middle-aged women at whom the book will be targeted. And the environment will be reminiscent of the setting of the book.

2. Is your immediate environment conducive to creating? I don't mean that you should suddenly take up feng shui, but are you surrounding yourself with creative people and creative influences? Competing with others is a powerful trigger to producing better ideas, which is why creative 'clusters' like Silicon Valley appear. Bearing in mind what Richard Florida describes as defining features of creative centres could it be time to move from Milton Keynes to Manchester?

---

eureka!

Unconscious Wildfire

In this book, I have described several different ways in which we make sense of the world, through analytical, emotional and creative intelligence, through the idea of constructs – how things are similar and how they are different, through memories, stories, the imagination and metaphors. These sense-making devices travel across conscious and unconscious neurons. I have also emphasised commonality – the extent to which we are similar to one another and how the skills and orientations of creative intelligence can be used in any context.

I have no doubt too, that later on in this century, neuroscientists will find out a great deal more about how our brains work, and that the knowledge will include features of the unconscious that we all share in common – in which case, Jung's idea of a collective unconscious could be quite viable, but perhaps not in quite the form he described. For now, though, I want to revert to the fundamental idea of constructs, and of this basic unit of making sense of ideas through similarity and difference. Ideas that spread like wildfire have a comforting familiarity to people in some ways; aspects of their form are readily identifiable and knowable. But there is also an apparently different, strange and new element about them too. To take a wildfire idea that is current at the time of writing, consider the Lord of the Rings trilogy, which has been made into three oscar-winning movies. The stories are familiar to most people, even if they haven't read them, but the cinematographic treatment of them is spectacular and new. What is reassuringly familiar about your idea and what is inventive and new?

10

The Future:
The Giant Wakes

Believing ~ Immersing ~ Idea generating ~ Creating a Vision ~ Reality-checking ~ Piloting ~ Realising

This chapter is about realising.

Eureka has covered many ideas and suggestions for building creative intelligence and making your ideas happen. Creativity and innovation are complex subjects, open to lots of different interpretations and full of contradictions. So I want this parting shot to be a useful and optimistic summing up of the ideas and suggestions in this book, describing how you, as an individual, can use them in the future, and the implications of using them in the world at large.

But first I want to consider an important question:

Can Absolutely Everyone be Creative?

We established early on in *eureka* that motivation and creativity are extremely closely linked. A key characteristic of highly creative people is the extent to which they immerse themselves totally in their subjects.

David McClelland, a Harvard Professor of Psychology, researched and wrote extensively about the psychology of motivation. He identified three key areas of motivation in adult life: the need for achievement – that is, making and producing things, what much of this book is about; the need for power – that is, exerting influence through others, what management books are often about; and the need for affiliation – that is, creating successful relationships, what a book like *Emotional Intelligence* is largely about.

McClelland speculated that these needs could develop very early in childhood. His research showed that adults who, as babies, had experienced quite structured approaches to feeding and toilet training, and developed a sense of what he called 'progressive mastery', tended to show quite a high need for achievement. No surprises there, then. The children of parents in groups where loss of power and oppression were high (immigrants, for instance) tended to develop a high power drive. This was also the case where parents were liberal about expressions of sex and aggression in childhood. Presumably the need for power is linked to asserting identity, which liberal parents encourage, exerting a low level of control over their children. I suspect most of us can recall occasions, on meeting a parent and child, where we experience a strong urge to say, 'Hello and nice to meet your child, the tyrant'!

Now I am very glad that there are people around who have a strong need for power. Where would we find many of our business and government leaders otherwise? It is important to realise, too, that, individually, we are likely to possess all three of these needs – but to different degrees. And while I would like to believe that all of us have the potential to be creative, some of us might just not be motivated to be so. It may be far more important for us, say, to be exercising power through managing people who create and innovate. For organisations like the BBC, understanding and tolerance of the differences between managers (with a strong need for power) and creatives (with a strong need for achievement) is something to strive for.

And of course what all of this boils down to is understanding one another a bit better. Politics and business would probably rub along a lot better if 'high need for power' politicians and 'high need for achievement' business leaders had frank conversations about their backgrounds, defining their experiences and motivations. I'm not going all touchy-feely here; it is just that there is great value in establishing informal dialogue.

This difference in individual motivation is significant. If you have a high need for achievement – which many creative people do, in my experience – you may feel quite frustrated and unsettled when you are not working on something creative. You also may find it impossible to understand where more managerial types are coming from when they help you implement your ideas. I don't know where these needs come from, but it seems logical that if we are praised and encouraged for achieving when we are young, we will want to repeat whatever behaviour that stimulates such positive feedback. There is very likely to be a compensatory element too; a friend told me that he writes books almost continuously because the activity gives him a sense of clarity, structure and order that was totally missing, he felt, from his upbringing.

So, while the urge to create is natural to all of us, some of us want to do it a lot more than others. After all, through selling what we create, we have developed capitalism.

Key eureka Ideas

Here, then, is a summing up of the most important ideas in this book, describing how you can take them away and use them in your own life and how they might affect the world at large. Or how to get that sleeping giant, Creativity, awake, barn-storming and roaring around the place.

Recognising creative intelligence

Early on in *eureka*, I put forward the case for creative intelli-gence, describing it as a set of skills using thoughts, emotions, imagination and the unconscious, as well as the conscious mind. I described it as being both a mindset – a way of habitually responding to things – and a process, which I described as a creativity spiral. Each chapter of this book has reflected a stage, or stages, in this spiral.

I suggested that you may have more creative intelligence than you realise, because it is not something that our education system seeks to identify and develop. Knowing how and where you want to make your ideas happen involves broadening your ideas about traditional intelligence and looking at what you love doing.

In *eureka*, I view people as having at least three types of intelligence: traditional IQ, emotional IQ and creative IQ. These three interact, and are inextricably linked with one another, in the same way that we now know the mind and the body are inextricably linked. You may have been shortchanging yourself in your own estimates of your intelligence, because you have confined it to traditional measurement systems.

Many perspectives might shift usefully in the world at large, if we viewed one another as being creatively intelligent. In the prison system, it is now widely acknowledged that 'thinking skills' courses do little to help rehabilitate offenders (although I think it is useful to teach these skills in other contexts). What seems to help prisoners above all else is skills-training, which help them become employable and do a job. Through this, their creative intelligence is recognised, endorsed and rewarded by society; the rehabilitated then mix with a different group of people as a result.

In running organisations with creative intelligence, unusual people would be recruited. The boards of NHS Trusts, for instance, would have rogue members who knew little initially about the health service, but held impressive records for creative problem-solving matters in complex environments. There would be far greater cross-over between the private and public sector, with innovative thinkers getting opportunities to take their approaches into very different contexts. A creatively intelligent approach is to say 'we don't want people like us around here; we want mavericks who question, challenge and offer unexpected alternatives'.

Full-on engagement

I've tried to avoid preaching about this, but it is undoubtedly full-on engagement that generates brilliant ideas and makes them happen. Through immersing ourselves totally in a subject area, we develop skills, mastery and the more unconscious, tacit, know-how. You are far more likely to have great ideas in a subject area when your skill and knowledge level is high, and you are more likely to be tenacious about your ideas, fuelled by self-belief.

I described a state called 'flow' where we are fully engaged with what we are doing, and feel extremely motivated. Obviously a way to be happier in life is to maximise the amount of time you spend in 'flow' and how much better if this can be the way you earn a living much of the time, too!

This notion of 'full-on engagement' is very relevant to today's world, with its ever-increasing demands on people's attention. How we manage our own and other people's attention spans is a fascinating question. For example, the teacher who has a couple of children with poor attention skills in her class is going to be under extra pressure if she has to get children finishing writing and maths exercise in a set time period. Her job might be much easier if, instead, during the early years of schooling, she focuses purely on getting her class to engage their attention fully on activities they undertake, rather than worrying about pressure to finish exercises in a relatively short time span. In my view, what is much overlooked in the school curriculum is the ability to engage with something fully, see it through to its completion and experience the accompanying sense of achievement from doing so. We may be overlooking the importance of teaching our children how to direct their attention, and how to be discerning about it.

Full-on engagement is risky, of course, because people may make fun of, reject and ridicule us because we care about something. But it's worth remembering that the post-modern, 'whatever' attitude is ultimately a defensive one; if you appear to care about nothing at all, then nobody can 'get you'. Does such a defensive position make life enjoyable?

The value of the unconscious

Scary though it may be, you can develop your creative intelligence by dropping any illusions you may have that you are in total conscious control. You ain't. But your unconscious mind need not be a saboteur whose desires you struggle to conceal. It is a powerful repository for your memories, on which your imaginings will be based. It can send your conscious mind very useful information and clarify and synthesise your ideas overnight, or, like Archimedes, when you are relaxing in the bath . . . We can give our conscious attention the task of feeding the unconscious through different experiences, environments and drift-time.

The unconscious is also vital to consider in terms of how we make sense of things: through metaphor, stories and archetypes. We may be prone to electing leaders who remind us of coherent archetypes, like Tony Blair, and resistant to electing those who are not recognisably placeable as archetypes. And we may be prone to unconscious fantasies about these leaders:

in the UK, when Tony Blair and New Labour came to power, the atmosphere was euphoric. Unconsciously, perhaps, many of us thought our saviour had arrived. Now he has revealed himself to be only human, so how can he fail to disappoint?

But it is in learning and education that the scope of valuing the unconscious gets really exciting. Its value is incorporated into the principles of what's been called Integrative Learning, Superlearning, Accelerated Learning or Suggestopeadia. These ideas were introduced by a Bulgarian called Geogi Lozanov back in 1950. Lozanov believed that the great majority of us were learning at between one-half and one-fifth of our natural capacity. This was due to the way we viewed learning, societally, as something unpleasant, confined to our traditional IQ and demanding great effort. Instead, we should remember that, as babies, we learn with our whole bodies, and total capacity – in a way that includes different intelligences, emotions, imaginings and drives.

Integrative learning claims that individuals learn through different channels. Many of us learn through visual processing – in other words, through watching. Doodlers are often big on visual learning. Some learn though auditory processing, like the child who loves to hear a bedtime story and concentrate entirely on listening, rather than looking at the pictures that might accompany the story. We also learn through kinaesthetic processing, a way of experiencing things through bodily sensation. The child who loves playing with water and sand springs to mind here. Some of us are very print-oriented – an approach that is fostered greatly by traditional education, while others are very group-orientated; we learn through discussion and our own output as well as input. (Yes, that's the child who's always being told to be quiet in class.)

A school in an economically deprived area of Chicago introduced the principles of Integrative Learning to its teachers, many of whom were very experienced and sceptical. Peter Kline, author of *The Everyday Genius*, led the initiative. The results were impressive. School attendance rose to 94% – a very high figure for a deprived inner-city school. At the end of the first year, students advancing a whole academic year in reading increased 103% over the previous year, while for reading and maths combined, the advance was 83% over the previous year. Peter Kline describes some really imaginative approaches in his book which encapsulate what Integrative Learning is about:

Act the inventor: in science lessons, students were asked to come as different famous scientists, like Darwin, Edison, Einstein and Newton, for instance. They were also asked to beef up on the background of the individuals – that is, to find interesting facts about them. Then they played a ball game where, when a student caught the ball, they revealed an interesting fact about the scientist. At first, not all students were equipped with many facts, but after the game became a regular event, they all began to turn up well prepared. Rather than it being merely a game that was about being good at science, the facts they learned enabled the students to play the ball game well.

Rap the science: students would be presented with a paper on a scientific experiment that they could read and listen to. Then they would split into groups and work out how they would rap sections of the paper. All the groups would come together and create a scientific rap symphony. By swapping sections, they could learn about every part of the experiment. Percussion instruments could be brought in to make the sections go with more of a swing.

History as Opera: though it is not fashionable to teach history as stories, it is surely the most effective way to engage children. Just hearing about what some historical interpretation says about a culture's values invariably has a big 'so what?' quality about it – rather like the post-modern philosophy from which it originates. When history (and, more obviously, literature) is told as stories, all sorts of dramatic possibilities arise. Students can put on costumes as different historical characters, and set defining moments in history to music, either making their own, or choosing suitable background theme music. They can script these moments, or even set them to music themselves and make an opera. This is great fun, intensely memorable and wondrously creative.

Groovy Grammar: learning rules of grammar by rote is not very meaningful. Whether a word is a verb, noun or adjective is always relevant to its meaning in a sentence. In this game, each part of a student's body becomes a verb, noun, adjective or adverb; for instance, an arm might be a verb, the head, a noun; the left shoulder, an adjective; the right shoulder, an adverb; the students could construct sentences by saying a word of their choice and moving the specific part of the body to touch another student. So 'the beautiful cat sat slowly on the mat' would involve a left shoulder from one student moving to the head of another student, moving to the arm of a third student, and so on. This is a creative memory aid.

Move the molecule: This game makes abstract ideas real by encouraging students to move as if they are the molecules of different solids, liquids and gases, and uses appropriate music to go with each movement. This reminds me of a contemporary dance class in my first year at university, where the teacher urged us to become packets of crisps. A down-to-earth and direct Scottish student, Stuart Cosgrove, piped up from the back row with: 'Eh, what flavour am I, miss?'

These approaches take a lot of the conscious effort out of learning. They recognise that students learn both unconsciously and consciously, and that body and mind are integrated and emotions and imagination matter as much as the more analytical, rational aspects of learning.

The power of vision

Much is written in self-help literature about low self-esteem and overcoming the fear of failure. Positive thinking can help deal with these problems, although they may never go away entirely, but it works better if it is in the shape of a vision, something that you imagine you would like to achieve. It needn't be a specific, tangible goal, but something that is sensory, which you can see, hear, smell, feel or experience in some way. You are always going to need to check your vision with reality, but the more vivid and detailed it is, and the more you focus your attention on it, the more likely it is to be realised.

In organisational life and government, the power of collective vision cannot be underestimated. Strategy and policy changes are frequently introduced in terms that imply that recipients are responding in a purely rational manner. Their feelings and fantasies, the stuff that 'vision' incorporates, are frequently overlooked. No wonder company changes meet overt and covert resistance, and are destined to fail. Just one question is overlooked here: what vision do these changes fit in with and how will people respond emotionally and imaginatively to them?

Engaging with criticism

Getting ideas produced is largely about balancing your vision with the feedback or criticism you get. Vision and self-belief help you ignore criticism that comes from jealousy and rivalry, and to constructively use the criticism that comes from the informed, the helpful and the wise. And they will include customers and clients. I am a great believer in desensitising yourself to criticism if you are very sensitive to it and desperately want to do well. Do this by putting yourself into situations where you get a lot of it, and where you can become discerning about what is useful and what is not. People who criticise readily are most useful; after all, they are at least engaged with what you are doing and giving you an impetus to recreate. They are not sitting on the sidelines and saying 'whatever'.

Organisational learning and leadership programmes where individuals get criticism from people who they interact with at all levels in the organisation seem to prove very useful. But really this only works if the CEO and others at top director level all swallow the same medicine. People become sceptical if a programme never reaches the top of an organisation. Balanced against getting feedback from the organisation, the truth – unpalatable for some of us – is that a lot of decisions are best taken by a small, stakeholding group of well-informed experts. Getting widespread input on decisions is often unwieldy and slow, and the naïve may overlook influences like political expediency in the public sector, and shareholder value in the private one.

Soft thinking

Soft thinking skills are about flexibility regarding how we think consciously, rather than rigidity. They increase options, bring creative solutions to problems and help people use their minds better. These thinking skills can be used on any subject under the sun, which is why they could be useful if taught extensively in schools, colleges and organisations.

My favourite idea in the entire psychological canon, because of its usefulness, is that of constructs, as described in Chapter Six. Where you are trying to implement an idea and encountering a lot of resistance – either from individuals, departments or entire organisations – then using constructs to sort out where you and they are coming from, and whether there is a possibility of you both moving to a third place together, keeps your idea moving. It may move to that third place or take you off in an entirely different direction. Identifying and discussing constructs are useful in any negotiating context

– in buying a house, industrial relations, acquisitions and mergers, or even world peace . . .

I have emphasised the overlap between learning and creativity in *eureka* and thought it might be useful to describe how soft thinking skills can be used for studying. Below are techniques for adults and children.

STAGE 42

The eureka programme: creative studying

1. Creating mind maps or spider webs of subject areas will help clarify relationships and contexts.
   Associating facts with mental pictures, like 1066 and the Battle of Hastings with lots of bloody bodies lying on a cliff-top, for instance, is a key memory technique. Prototyping or piloting essays is essential. Making hypothetical exam answers will keep you engaged in studying and is a good dry run for your actual exams. After all, performance on the day is about output, not input.

2. Integrative learning offers the following approach for studying text books quickly and efficiently. Look at a book's chapter headings to see what areas are covered and in what format. Then read the summaries of each chapter. With blank paper and pen, draw the key concepts that are covered by the book. Then you are in a fine position to know where you need to go to cover specific subjects in greater depth. It was only until I was half-way through a PhD that I learnt of this technique, and I expect there are a lot of other PhD students out there who could do with knowing it. Its basis is the same as that of creative intelligence: get a feel for the whole area

first, its patterns and structures, and then choose where to zoom in.

3. Another way in which integrative learning is applied is through what has been called the brain gym. These are physical exercises that are said to help the brain function more effectively and to help to reinvigorate it during long periods of study. They tap into the nervous system and include exercises like the following.

Brain buttons: standing up, with one hand on your navel to feel your centre of gravity, take your other hand and gently massage the area just below your shoulder bone on either side of your breast bone. This stimulates circulation through the carotid arteries to your brain.

Cross walking: this is cross-lateral walking on the spot, bringing your right elbow to your left knee, and your left elbow to your right knee. It should improve communication between the two hemispheres of your brain.

Hook ups: Stand with your ankles crossed, then bring your arms across the front of your body, bent at the elbows, linking your fingers to your hands cross over. Put your tongue just behind the ridge at the back of your top teeth. Spend two minutes like this – it should make you feel more focussed and integrated.

Lazy 8s: this is a paper and pen exercise to help your writing flow more freely. On a large piece of paper, just doodle repeatedly the figure 8, starting at the centre and letting the pen repeatedly flow over the same shape without it leaving the page. This is good to ease stress, apparently.

Creators keep themselves motivated through giving themselves a sense of their performance and progress. Before big exams, you or your children can learn to be your own best coaches by planning your revision, dividing it up into smaller chunks, and monitoring your perform-ance through a diary or a journal. You may also find it useful to record how you feel about your progress, and to build in periods of reflection time about this.

Stories as meaning

Through emphasising stories as a way of selling ideas, I hope I have convinced you that influencing others can be a highly creative, imaginative and exciting activity. It involves under-standing how we make sense of the world, fundamentally, and appreciating how much common understanding we share. In the world at large, people are likely to be far more receptive to policy and organisational changes if they understand where they fit in 'their story so far'.

In education, also, the story form could make a far greater creative contribution.

Philip Pullman, the literary award-winning children's author, gave a memorable and controversial speech at the 2003 *Sunday Times* Oxford Literary Festival in which he said:

> I want to champion teaching as telling stories. I think we should bring back storytelling into our classrooms and do it at once. And I mean all kinds of stories: not just that every teacher should have a repertoire of fairy tales or ghost stories that they can bring out on a wet Friday afternoon, or when the video breaks down on a field study weekend – though I do mean that, and in spades; but true stories about historical events, about music and musicians, about engineers and engineering, about archae-ology, about science, about the theatre, about politics, about exploration, about art – in fact stories about every kind of human activity.
>
> And when you are telling a story, you need to let the

*story take its own time. Never mind these programmes
and units and key stages: to hell with them. There's no
human meaning in rubbish like that. If the children want
to go on listening, then go on telling.*

*And when you come to the end of the story, stop. Let
it do its own work in its own time; don't tear it into rags
by making the poor children analyse, and comment, and
compare, and interpret. The world is full of stories, full
of true nourishments for the heart and the mind and the
imagination; and this true nourishment is lying all around
our children, untouched, and they're being force-fed on
ashes and sawdust and potato peelings.*

How inspiring is that, and clock those metaphors . . .

Unconscious influences: groups and viruses

I couldn't decide, when naming this idea, whether to call it
'invisible influences' or 'unconscious influences'. I wanted to
describe the processes that go on in groups, whereby good
ideas get damned irretrievably, or are never expressed, and the
several influences that come together to make an idea virally
popular and successful, as described in Chapters Eight and
Nine. In the end, I decided that these significant influences are
more unconscious than invisible – because we can usually see
the cynical response of the individual who prevents anyone else
in a group daring to suggest new ideas, even though we may
not be aware consciously that this is how they contaminate
creative potential. Similarly, we can walk around a town and
see passers-by and think 'this looks like an interesting place to
live' without realising, consciously, how this environment may
be fostering creativity.

It seems to me that if our leaders understood a little more
about how people make sense of the world via their imaginations and emotions as well as their reasoning, they would act

with greater prudence. For instance, a leader who generates a lot of saviour fantasies in people guards against appearing too sanctimonious or over-championing of the moral high ground. She or he would know they would be better placed to encourage people to take a more realistic perspective.

As well as helping spread our ideas, for us as individuals, living a 'networked life' through people and computers, is simply much more fulfilling in my view. Communities of interests rather than geographical communities now provide us with our social glue. And they offer endless chances to experience those warm glows of self-endorsement that come from thinking 'here is a person who thinks just like me about this. I am not alone'!

Final Word

One quote has stuck in my mind from the outset of researching this subject. An academic – somewhere in America probably – started their paper with the announcement that 'Creativity isn' easy'. Now I won't reveal to you how often my thoughts have strayed to this quote during the writing of this book, but I can tell you that I think the academic was right.

No, I'm not asking for a medal, but this is not a subject that can be dealt with by prescribing 10 steps to get it. It defies linear analysis and anyone who conveys it as such is doing creativity a disservice. Successful creativity and innovation require both attitude and process, as described in my creativity spiral, with behaviour being revisited and repeated.

In *eureka*, I've emphasised how to make your brilliant ideas happen by playing three useful roles: those of creator, researcher and critic. I've also emphasised the importance of engagement and discussion. Please engage and discuss with me at www.philippadavies.co.uk if you wish to.

Thank you for staying with me and I hope you end *eureka*

feeling inspired. Just remember, also, the power of the bath. Like Archimedes, if you are feeling jaded, then run a deep one.

And when that eureka moment explodes, and you burst out of the bathroom, well . . . please remember that others may react better to a towel . . .